GOD COMFORTS
HIS PEOPLE

THE STORY BIBLE SERIES

1. *God's Family* tells the story of creation, God's promises to Abraham's family, and the adventures of Joseph.

2. *God Rescues His People* tells about Israel's escape from Egypt, Moses and the Ten Commandments, and the wandering in the wilderness.

3. *God Gives the Land* tells the story of Joshua, the adventures of the judges, and the story of Ruth.

4. *God's Chosen King* tells about Samuel, Saul, and David, God's promises to David's family, and the Psalms.

5. *God's Wisdom and Power* tells about the glorious reign of Solomon, the wonderful works of Elijah and Elisha, and the Proverbs and the Song of Songs.

6. *God's Justice* tells the story of the prophets Amos, Hosea, Isaiah, and Jeremiah and their messages of God's judgment and mercy.

7. *God Comforts His People* tells about God's people in exile, their return to the land, and the adventures of Esther and Daniel.

Additional books in the series will tell stories from the New Testament.

Story Bible Series, Book 7

GOD COMFORTS HIS PEOPLE

Stories of God and His People from Ezekiel, Lamentations, Isaiah, Ezra, Haggai, Zechariah, Obadiah, Malachi, Joel, Nehemiah, Esther, Jonah, Job, Ecclesiastes, and Daniel

Retold by Eve B. MacMaster
Illustrated by James Converse

HERALD PRESS
Scottdale, Pennsylvania
Kitchener, Ontario
1985

Library of Congress Cataloging in Publication Data

MacMaster, Eve, 1942-
    God comforts his people.

    (Story Bible series ; bk. 7)
    Summary: Presents stories about God's people
in exile and their return to the land, as given
in Ezekiel, Ecclesiastes, Daniel, and Twelve
other books of the Old Testament.
    1. Bible stories, English—O.T.   Prophets.
2. Bible stories, English—O.T.   Hagiographa.
[1. Bible stories—O.T.]   I. Converse, James,
ill.   II. Bible. O.T.   III. Title.   IV. Series.
BS551.2.M294   1985   221.9'505   85-835
ISBN 0-8361-3393-5 (pbk.)

GOD COMFORTS HIS PEOPLE
Copyright © 1985 by Herald Press, Scottdale, Pa. 15683
        Published simultaneously in Canada by Herald Press,
        Kitchener, Ont. N2G 4M5. All rights reserved.
Library of Congress Catalog Card Number: 85-835
International Standard Book Number: 0-8361-3393-5
Printed in the United States of America
Design: Alice B. Shetler

90 89 88 87 86 85 10 9 8 7 6 5 4 3 2 1

The Story of This Book

Several years ago I was looking for a Bible story book to read to my children. I wanted one that was complete, without tacked-on morals or a denominational interpretation. I wanted one that was faithful to the Bible and fun to read. I couldn't find what I was looking for.

With the encouragement of my husband, Richard MacMaster, I approached Herald Press with the idea of the series: a retelling of the whole Bible with nothing added and nothing subtracted, just following the story line through the Old and New Testaments.

The people at Herald Press were agreeable and enthusiastic and gave much valuable advice, especially book editor Paul M. Schrock.

At his suggestion, I asked some academic and professional people in our community to check the stories for style and accuracy. Members of the advisory committee, who have kindly volunteered their time, include Bible professors George R. Brunk III, Ronald D. Guengerich, G. Irvin Lehman, and Kenneth Seitz; and childhood curriculum and librarian specialists Elsie E. Lehman and A. Arlene Bumbaugh.

I hope this series will lead its readers to the original, for no retelling is a substitute for the Bible itself. The Bible is actually a collection of books written over a long period of time in a variety of forms. It has been translated and retold in every generation because people everywhere want to know what God is like.

The main character in every story is God. The plot of every story is God's activity among his people: creating, saving, fighting, reigning, and doing works of wisdom and power, justice and mercy.

The first book in the series is *God's Family*. It tells stories about God the Creator.

The second book is *God Rescues His People*. It tells stories about God the Savior.

The third book is *God Gives the Land*. It tells stories about God the warrior.

The fourth book, *God's Chosen King*, tells stories about God the true King.

The fifth book, *God's Wisdom and Power*, tells stories about God, the source of wisdom and power.

The sixth book, *God's Justice*, tells stories about God the righteous Judge.

This book, *God Comforts His People*, tells stories about God's mercy to his people in exile. It includes the adventures of Daniel and Esther in Babylon and Persia and the story of the return to the land of Judah. In the midst of exile, danger, and persecution God comforts his people with messages of hope and rescues them from the power of their enemies.

This volume is dedicated to the people today who bring God's comfort and hope to a troubled world.

—Eve MacMaster
Bridgewater, Virginia
St. Nicholas Day, 1984

Contents

God Comforts His People

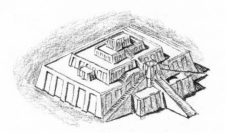

1

Exiles in Babylon

2 Kings 24; 2 Chronicles 36; Jeremiah 27—29

BABYLON! What could be greater than the capital city of the strongest kingdom on earth?

Babylon! What could be more frightening than the power of Nebuchadnezzar, king of Babylon?

The captives from Judah were arriving in Babylon after a long, wearying journey. They shuddered when they thought of the dangers that waited for them in this strange foreign city.

The men, women, and children from Judah looked like a defeated army. They numbered seven thousand—priests and nobles, government officials, skilled workers, and their king, Jehoiachin, with his five sons.

Nebuchadnezzar's army had invaded the land of Judah to punish the Israelites for rebelling against him. His soldiers took the leading citizens captive and brought them back to Babylon to keep them from making more trouble for the empire.

So now, after weeks of travel, here they were, exiles from Judah, strangers in Babylon.

The exiles saw the glory of Babylon, the old city that Nebuchadnezzar had enlarged and improved with the wealth from the nations he conquered. They saw the magnificent royal palace with its famous hanging gardens, one of the seven wonders of the ancient world. They noticed that the walls of Babylon were stronger and thicker than the walls of Jerusalem, their own beloved city back in Judah.

As the captives walked through the straight, broad streets of Babylon, they noticed temples everywhere. There were temples to the sun, to the moon, the stars, and the planets; temples to the goddess Ishtar and to the gods Bel and Nebo. In the center of the city, rising high above all other buildings, was the great ziggurat-temple of Marduk, god of Babylon.

The rulers and people of Babylon treated the exiles kindly and helped them find places to live. Jehoiachin and his sons were kept under close guard, but the other Israelites were allowed to settle in towns outside the capital.

The Israelites felt homesick. They didn't like their new brick houses; they preferred their stone houses back in Judah. They didn't like the flat Tigris-Euphrates Valley; they missed the rocky hills around Jerusalem.

One day news arrived from home. Nebuchadnezzar had put Jehoiachin's uncle Mattaniah on the throne of Judah. He had renamed the new king Zedekiah and made him promise to be loyal to Babylon.

Another day the prophet Jeremiah sent a letter from Jerusalem, telling the exiles to build houses and settle down, to plant gardens and raise their families in Babylon. Jeremiah said the exile would last seventy years.

Seventy years! The exiles refused to believe Jeremiah's prophecy. They preferred to listen to other prophets who encouraged them to believe that they would soon be on their way home.

As the years passed, many of the exiles settled in the town of Tel Abib beside the Chebar Canal, a few miles south of Babylon. Among them was a young priest named Ezekiel. His name meant "God strengthens," and one day the Lord God of Israel strengthened Ezekiel in a strange and wonderful way.

2

God Strengthens Ezekiel

Ezekiel 1—3

IT was an ordinary summer day in the fifth year of the exile when Ezekiel noticed the north wind blowing a large storm cloud toward him. Inside the cloud was a mass of fire; all around it the sky glowed with a bright, unearthly light.

As the cloud came near, Ezekiel could see four creatures in the fire. They were gold and shiny, like polished bronze. They stood up like human beings, but their feet were round like cattle. Each creature had four wings, four hands, and four faces. The faces in front were human faces; the

15

faces on the right were lions' faces; the faces on the left were bulls' faces; and the faces in back were eagles' faces.

Two of each creature's wings hung down beside their hands while the other two wings were spread out, touching the tips of the other creatures' wings.

When the creatures moved, they moved together without turning their heads or their bodies, for they could look in all four directions at once.

As the strange creatures moved closer to Ezekiel, he noticed four enormous wheels, one beside each creature. Within each wheel was another wheel, so each could move in all four directions without turning. The wheels sparkled like jewels, and their outside rims were full of watching eyes.

The creatures moved, and the wheels moved with them. As they rose together into the air, their wings made a sound like the roar of the ocean. Ezekiel watched them go up, and way above them he saw a great dome, shining like ice in the sunlight.

When the creatures and the wheels suddenly stopped in the middle of the air, Ezekiel saw something above the shining dome. It looked like a throne made of bright blue sapphire. Sitting high up on the throne was someone who looked like a human being, someone shining like golden bronze in the middle of the fire, with a glow as bright as a rainbow all around him.

It was the glory of the Lord, and when he saw it, Ezekiel threw himself face downward to the ground.

"O man!" said a voice. "Stand up. I have something to say to you."

As the voice spoke, Ezekiel felt the Spirit of God come into him and lift him to his feet.

"O man," repeated the voice. "I'm sending you to the people of Israel. They're a stubborn, hardhearted nation. They've rebelled against me, just as their ancestors did. Whether or not they pay attention to you, when I send you to them, they'll realize that a prophet has been among them.

"Don't be afraid of them, son of man. Don't be afraid of their words. They'll treat you cruelly and make you feel as though you're sitting on top of thorns and scorpions. But don't be afraid of anything they say, for they're a rebellious nation. Just speak my words to them.

"As for you, O man, listen to what I say. Don't be a rebel like them. Now open your mouth and eat whatever I give you."

Ezekiel saw something like a hand reaching out to him, holding a scroll. The hand unrolled the scroll in front of him, and he saw words written all over both sides—words of sorrow and disaster.

"O man," said the Lord. "Eat what's in front of you! Eat this scroll and then go speak to the Israelites!"

Ezekiel opened his mouth and took the scroll onto his tongue.

"Swallow it!" commanded the Lord.

Ezekiel swallowed the scroll. In his mouth it became as sweet as honey.

"O man," said the Lord. "Go to the people of Israel and tell them what I have to say to them. I'm not sending you to foreigners who speak a strange and difficult language. If I sent you to foreigners, they'd pay attention to you. No, these Israelites will refuse to listen to you, because they refuse to listen to me. They're stubborn and rebellious.

"So now I'm going to strengthen you. I'll make

you as tough and as stubborn as they are. You'll become as hard as a diamond, as tough as flint. You won't be afraid of them.

"Just listen carefully, O man, and remember everything I tell you. Go to the exiles and speak. Whether or not they pay attention, tell them you're speaking the words of the Lord God!"

Then the Spirit of God lifted Ezekiel up and carried him away. Behind him Ezekiel could hear the great rushing sound of the winged creatures and the rumbling of the wheels as the glory of the Lord rose back up to heaven. He felt the power of the Lord on him like a heavy hand.

Then, suddenly, the vision was gone, and Ezekiel was home again among the exiles by the Chebar Canal. He felt angry and bitter, and for seven days he stayed in his house, exhausted by what he had seen and heard.

3

The Brick and the Hair

Ezekiel 3—7

SEVEN days after his first vision, Ezekiel heard from the Lord again.

"O man," said the Lord. "I'm making you a watchman for the Israelites. Warn them about the disaster that's coming. You're responsible for giving them my message!"

Then the power of the Lord came over Ezekiel, and the Lord said to him, "Get up and go out into the valley. I'll speak to you there."

Ezekiel did as the Lord commanded, and in the valley he saw the glory of the Lord. He fell down with his face to the ground.

The Spirit of God came to Ezekiel and lifted him up, and the Lord said to him, "Go home. Lock yourself inside your house. I'm going to make your tongue stick to the roof of your mouth so you won't be able to speak. I'll let you speak only when I have something for you to say."

Ezekiel went home and locked himself inside his house. Then the Lord spoke to him, giving him strange messages to act out in front of the people—messages of sorrow and disaster.

For the next four years Ezekiel spoke only when the Lord gave him a message. Like a watchman, he warned the people of the disaster that was coming. When he tried to say anything else, his tongue stuck to the roof of his mouth.

Every day Ezekiel went outside to the front of his house, where his neighbors could see him. There he acted out the messages the Lord gave him.

First he took a sun-dried brick and scratched some lines on it, in the form of a city. Then he pretended to be an invading army. He attacked the brick. He built watchtowers and siege ramps next to it. He rammed it with a battering ram. Then, while the exiles watched, Ezekiel lay on his side next to the brick. He lay down with ropes around him, nibbling a small piece of bread and sipping a little drink of water.

Every day for three hundred and ninety days Ezekiel came out of his house and lay on his left side next to the brick. Then for forty days he lay on his right side. After this, he glared at the brick and shook his fist at it and screamed at it.

Every day the Israelites went to Ezekiel's house to see what strange thing the prophet would do next.

They saw him take a razor and shave the hair from his head and his beard. They saw him sweep up the hair, weigh it on scales, and divide it into three equal piles. He carried one pile over to the brick and burned it. He took the second pile of hair and spread it around the brick and chopped it up with a sword. He threw the third pile into the air, scattering it in the wind. When some of the hair fell back to the ground, he

picked it up and threw some of it into the fire and wrapped some of it in the folds of his cloak.

The people wanted an explanation of Ezekiel's strange behavior. Finally Ezekiel spoke to them.

"Hear the word of the Lord!" he cried. "This brick is the city of Jerusalem! Jerusalem has rebelled against the Lord. Instead of living as the Lord has commanded, the people of Jerusalem worship idols and commit injustice. They lie and cheat and steal. They hurt the poor. They have no respect for the Lord and his temple.

"Because they have sinned against the Lord and each other, the Lord won't save them from their enemies. He's going to send an army to invade Judah, to attack Jerusalem. He'll use that army to punish the people.

"Jerusalem will suffer a terrible siege. The people of Israel will be punished for their sins. The days I was lying on my side are the years of their wickedness. They'll be trapped inside the city during the siege, as I was tied up with the ropes. They'll have only a little bread to eat and a little water to drink, as I did when I lay down beside the brick."

Then Ezekiel explained why he shaved off his hair. "The hair is the people of Jerusalem," he said. "One third of them will die inside the city from disease and starvation. Another third will be struck down by the swords of their enemies. The rest will be scattered in all directions, like the hair in the wind. Only a few will be saved.

"The ones who will be saved will be sorry for their sins. They'll turn back to the Lord. But all the rest must perish. No one can save Jerusalem."

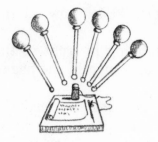

The Fall of Jerusalem

Ezekiel 8—33

ONE day about a year after Ezekiel first saw the glory of the Lord, he suddenly felt the power of the Lord come over him. He saw a being like a man, all fire from the waist down and shining like bronze from the waist up.

The Lord reached out and took Ezekiel by the hair, and the Spirit of God lifted him up and carried him in a vision to Jerusalem.

In the vision the Lord put Ezekiel down by the entrance of the temple, and he saw the glory of the Lord shining in front of the temple.

25

"O man!" said the Lord. "Look toward the north."

Ezekiel saw an idol standing in front of the temple of God: an image of Asherah, the pagan goddess of love.

"See what the people are doing!" cried the Lord. "They practice disgusting things here. They're driving me out of my temple. And there's more!"

He took Ezekiel to the outer courtyard of the temple and showed him a hole in the wall.

"Son of man," said the Lord. "Dig through the wall."

Ezekiel dug through the wall.

"Now go in," said the Lord. "Go in and see what filthy things they're doing."

Ezekiel crawled through the hole. He found himself inside the temple, in a room with walls covered with pictures of snakes and toads and lizards. These reptiles were the gods of Egypt. Seventy elders of Israel were standing in front of the pictures, holding incense burners and worshiping the idols.

"O man," said the Lord. "Did you see what's happening? They're worshiping idols inside my temple! They think I can't see them. And there's more!"

He took Ezekiel to the north gate of the temple, where he showed him some women sitting in the courtyard. They were worshiping Tammuz, the Babylonian fertility god.

"O man," said the Lord. "Do you see that? And there's even worse!"

He took Ezekiel to the inner courtyard and showed him some men standing by the entrance of the temple. They were facing away from the temple, bowing toward the east. They were worshiping the rising sun.

"O man, do you see that? They've filled the land with their crimes! They put their stink right up my nose! They come to my temple to insult me!"

Then Ezekiel heard the Lord shout, "Bring on the executioners! Let them come and destroy the city!"

Six men appeared with war clubs in their hands. With them was another man, dressed in white linen and carrying a pen, ink, and a writing tablet.

The men with the war clubs stopped beside the altar in the temple courtyard while the Lord spoke to the man in white.

"Go through the city," commanded the Lord. "Mark an X on the foreheads of the people who are sorry about what's going on—the ones who care about the Lord and his people."

Then the Lord spoke to the destroying angels, who were waiting with clubs in their hands.

"Follow the man in white," he told them. "Go through the city and strike all the people except the ones with the mark on their foreheads. Begin here at the temple."

The destroying angels struck the elders who were worshiping the sun. Then they went out into the city.

As soon as they had left, Ezekiel threw himself down onto the ground and cried out, "O Lord God, will you destroy everyone in the city?"

"The land is full of murder," answered the Lord. "The city is filled with injustice. These terrible crimes have to be punished. Jerusalem must be destroyed."

Then the man in white returned. "I've done as you commanded," he said.

Ezekiel looked up and saw the glory of the Lord rising from the temple. As he watched, the glory of the Lord left the temple and went away from Jerusalem.

Then the Spirit of God brought Ezekiel back to Babylon, and the vision faded away.

Ezekiel told the exiles everything he had seen and heard. He warned them over and over about the disaster that was coming.

But the exiles didn't pay any attention to Ezekiel's warnings. They didn't believe that Jerusalem would be destroyed. They didn't believe the temple would be ruined. They thought the glory of the Lord would stay in Jerusalem. They thought the Lord would save them from their enemies, no matter what crimes they committed.

Then one day in the winter of the ninth year of the exile, the Lord said to Ezekiel, "Son of man, write down today's date. For this is the day that the king of Babylon is beginning the siege of Jerusalem. The city is doomed. As a sign, I'm going to take away from you the most precious thing you have, the person you love the most. And when this happens, you must not cry or mourn."

That morning Ezekiel spoke to the people, and in the evening his wife died. She was the person he loved the most.

The next day Ezekiel didn't cry or mourn, and the people were amazed by his behavior.

"Why are you acting this way?" they asked. "What does it mean?"

Ezekiel answered, "The Lord is going to take away from you the most precious thing you have—the temple in Jerusalem. Your family and friends in Judah will be killed. You'll want to cry and mourn, but it will be no use."

Then the Lord said to Ezekiel, "A messenger will come with news from Jerusalem. When he arrives, I'll give you back the power of speech. You'll be able to talk whenever you wish."

While Ezekiel and the exiles waited for news from Jerusalem, Ezekiel spoke to them about God's plans to punish the nations. The proud city of Tyre and the great nation of Egypt would fall to the cruel soldiers of Nebuchadnezzar, king of Babylon.

The siege of Jerusalem lasted for a year and a half. Nebuchadnezzar's army was determined to punish Zedekiah for rebelling against Babylon. The people inside the city waited and waited for help, but help never came.

One evening Ezekiel felt the power of the Lord on him, and he realized that he could speak whenever he wished. The next day a messenger arrived at Tel Abib with the news: Jerusalem had been destroyed.

5

Who Will Comfort Jerusalem?

Lamentations

THE siege of Jerusalem was terrible. Nebuchadnezzar's army attacked the city with
towers, ramps, and battering rams. They cut off
all the supplies of food and water, so many people
inside the city died of disease and starvation.
When the soldiers finally broke through the wall,
they killed many more with their swords.

They set fire to the city, and the walls and the
temple collapsed into heaps of rubble. Nebuchadnezzar took all the valuable gold and silver
equipment from the temple of the Lord, and

when he returned to Babylon, he put it in the temple of Marduk, his god.

Many of the survivors of the siege were taken prisoner and forced to go to Babylon, joining the first group of exiles. Among them was Zedekiah, uncle of King Jehoiachin. No new king was set up in Zedekiah's place. The smoking ruins of the temple marked the end of the kingdom of Judah.

At first the Israelites thought that God had abandoned them to their enemies. Then they began to realize that they were being punished for their sins. Slowly they began to turn back to the Lord their God. They expressed these feelings of sorrow and shame by crying and mourning, in prayers and songs.

When the Israelites met together to worship the Lord, they sang some of these sad songs, called Lamentations.

Who Will Comfort Jerusalem?

How lonely lies the city,
   once so full of people.
Once great among nations,
   now she is like a widow.
Once a princess among cities,
   now she is a slave.

She cries all night;
   tears run down her cheeks.
She has nobody to comfort her;
   all her friends have turned against her.

See what happened to Jerusalem!
Is there any pain
   like my pain?
Listen, all you nations!
   Look at my pain!
My young men and women
   have gone into exile!

Look, Lord, how I suffer!
My heart is broken
   because of my sins!

The Lord Is Faithful

I thought my faith in the Lord
   was gone;
I thought only about
   my misery,
   my pain,
   and my suffering;
I thought about it all the time,
   and I felt depressed.

Then I remembered one thing
   that gave me hope:
The mercy of the Lord never ends;
his love goes on forever;
it is new every morning.
Great is his faithfulness!
The Lord is merciful;
he won't reject us forever.

O Lord, bring us back to you,
   and we will come back.

Restore your people, Lord!

Or have you rejected us
   completely?
Is there no limit
   to your anger?

6

The Valley of Dry Bones and the New Jerusalem

Ezekiel 34—48

ONE day after the fall of Jerusalem the power of the Lord came over Ezekiel, and the Spirit of God took him away and put him down in a valley. The bottom of the valley was covered with bones.

The Lord told Ezekiel to walk up and down the valley, and he saw that there was an enormous number of bones, and they were very dry.

"O man," said the Lord. "Can these bones come back to life?"

"Only you know, Lord God," answered Ezekiel.

Then the Lord said, "Prophesy to these bones!"

Ezekiel spoke to the bones as the Lord commanded him. "Dry bones!" he said, "Hear the word of the Lord! The Lord God says he's going to put the breath of life into you, and you will live. He'll put muscles and flesh on you and cover you with skin. You'll come back to life, and then you'll know that he is the Lord!"

As Ezekiel was speaking, he heard a noise—the sound of the bones rattling as they joined together. While Ezekiel watched, muscles and flesh appeared on the bones, and skin covered them. But there was no breath in the bodies.

"Son of man," said the Lord. "Prophesy to the wind!"

Ezekiel spoke to the wind, saying, "Come,

wind, come from the four corners of the earth and breathe life into these dead bodies. Let them live!"

The wind came and blew, and the breath of life entered the bodies. The bodies lived and stood on their feet, and the valley was full of them—a mighty army of people!

"O man," said the Lord. "These bones are the whole people of Israel. They say their bones are dried up and their life is gone. They're as hopeless as dead people. Now, go tell them that I'm going to raise them up and lead them home. I'm going to put my spirit into them, and they'll live again!

"I'll be like a good shepherd, taking care of my people. And some day I'll send a king like David to lead them. The nations will know what I am like.

"I punished them because of their sins, but I'll show pity on them and bless them. I'll bring them back to the land and give them new hearts. I'll remove their hearts of stone and give them hearts of flesh. I'll put my spirit in them so they can follow my teachings and obey my commandments. I'll never leave them again. I will be their God, and they will be my people."

Ezekiel shared this message of hope with the exiles. Then, a few years later, he again felt the power of the Lord, and he received another message of hope for the future.

The Lord carried Ezekiel in a vision to the land

of Israel. There he showed him a wonderful new temple in a glorious new Jerusalem.

As the Lord led him to the city, Ezekiel saw a man standing in the gateway, shining like golden bronze. He was holding a measuring line in his hand.

"O man," he said to Ezekiel. "Look closely and listen carefully, for you have been brought here to see things and tell the people about them."

The guide showed Ezekiel a new temple and led him through all its rooms, inside and out. While Ezekiel watched, he carefully measured each room.

Then they crossed the courtyard to the east gate, and Ezekiel saw the bright light of the glory of the Lord, and he heard the voice of the Lord. The whole earth was shining with the light of the glory of God.

Ezekiel threw himself down to the ground, and the light of the glory of the Lord passed through the east gate and into the temple. Then the Spirit of God lifted Ezekiel up and took him to the entrance of the temple. He saw that the whole temple was filled with the glory of the Lord.

"O man," said the voice of the Lord. "I will make my throne here among my people, and rule over them forever. Never again will they disgrace my holy name with their sins."

Then Ezekiel's guide took him outside and showed him a place where water was flowing from underneath the temple. As Ezekiel walked along, the water became a stream, and the stream grew wider and deeper, until finally it became a mighty river.

"This river flows down to the Jordan," explained the guide. "It fills the sea with fresh water. It is full of life wherever it flows. Animals and all kinds of fish live in the water, and all kinds of trees grow beside it. These are healing waters, for the plants that grow beside it heal all kinds of diseases."

Then the guide showed Ezekiel the gate of the new Jerusalem. "From now on," he said, "this city will be named 'The Lord Is Here!' "

These visions were signs of hope for God's people in exile, promises that one day the Lord would bring them back to life and give them a new temple in a new city where the Lord would always be with them.

7

God Comforts His People

Isaiah 40—66

ABOUT twenty-five years after the fall of Jerusalem, Nebuchadnezzar died, and his son Amel-Marduk became king of Babylon. Amel-Marduk was kind to Jehoiachin, king of Judah, and set him free from prison.

This was a sign of hope for the exiles. But then Amel-Marduk was overthrown by a cruel man named Nabonidus, and the exiles became discouraged again.

During the long years of the exile the priests and prophets of the Lord taught the people about

God and encouraged them to believe God's promises.

One of God's prophets spoke hopeful messages of comfort to the exiles. He said the time was coming when the Lord would lead his people back to the land. He would rescue them from exile in Babylon as he had once rescued them from slavery in Egypt.

The prophet spoke of God's decision to forgive his people.

"Comfort, comfort my people,"
   says your God.
"Speak kindly to Jerusalem
   and tell her this:

" 'Her time of service is ended;
   her sin is pardoned.
" 'She has received from the Lord's hand
   double punishment
   for all her crimes.' "

Clear a road through the wilderness
   for the Lord!
Straighten out a highway across the desert
   for our God!

Every valley will be lifted up;
   every mountain and hill
     will be brought down.
Every cliff will become a plain;
   every rough place
     will become smooth.

Then the glory of the Lord
    will be revealed!
Everyone will see it,
    for the Lord himself has spoken!

This messenger of hope said that the Lord was going to come in power like a mighty king, but gently like a shepherd. He would gather the baby lambs in his arms and carry them next to his heart.

The Lord was going to judge all nations. He was going to destroy the worthless gods of Babylon; he was going to pull down the power of Babylon and lift up the power of Persia. He was going to use Cyrus, king of Persia, to bring the exiles back to Judah.

In the future, said the prophet, the nations of the earth would come to Jerusalem to learn about the Lord. The new Israel would be God's servant, a light to the nations, showing them the way to salvation.

A mysterious person called the Servant of the Lord would suffer for the sins of the people. He would be despised and rejected. He would be sacrificed like a lamb to carry away the sins of the world.

God's ways are impossible for human beings to understand, said the prophet, but the word of the Lord always comes true. We can believe his promises.

God Restores His People

8

Return to Judah

Ezra 1—3

AS time passed, the little children who went into exile grew up and had children of their own. Those children had no memory of Jerusalem or the land of Judah. Their parents and grandparents told them about the temple and about God's promises to restore his people.

After the death of Nebuchadnezzar, the power of Babylon grew weak. New nations rose in the East, in the mountains of Media and Persia. A Persian king named Cyrus united the Persian tribes, conquered the Medes, and led his army as far as the Greek kingdoms of Asia Minor. And then, as the Lord had promised, mighty Babylon fell to the power of Cyrus.

Cyrus built up a new empire even greater than the empire of Nebuchadnezzar. But he was kind to the nations he conquered. He didn't send the people into exile, but allowed them to live in their own lands and worship their own gods.

The year after Cyrus conquered Babylon, the Lord inspired him to help the exiles from Judah. Cyrus sent messengers to announce the news to the exiles.

"Hear the word of Cyrus, king of Persia!" cried the royal messengers. "Cyrus says: 'The Lord, the God of heaven, has made me ruler of all the kingdoms of the earth. He has told me to build a house for him in the city of Jerusalem.

" 'Now you people go up to Jerusalem and rebuild the temple. I'll order your neighbors in Babylon to help you, to give you silver and gold, food and pack animals for your journey, and offerings for the temple of the Lord.' "

When the exiles heard this news, God inspired many of them to answer the call to return to Jerusalem. But most of them decided to remain in Babylon, for they had become rich farmers, merchants, and bankers. The journey to Judah would be dangerous and expensive, and Babylon was a safer and more comfortable place to live.

But hundreds of priests and heads of families made plans to return. Their leader was

Sheshbazzar, a prince of the royal family.

Cyrus took the gold and silver bowls, cups, plates, and dishes that Nebuchadnezzar had removed from the Lord's temple and gave them to the exiles who were planning to return. Some of the Babylonians gave them gifts of silver and gold, food for the journey, mules, camels, and donkeys to carry their baggage, and offerings for the temple of the Lord.

Hundreds of men, women, and children left Babylon and traveled the eight hundred miles to the land of Judah. When they arrived in Jerusalem, they found a ruined city in a barren land. The walls of Jerusalem were reduced to heaps of rubble, black from the smoke of the fires

that had destroyed the city. Only a few poor peasants were left in the city. Enemies threatened on every side.

After the fall of Jerusalem, foreigners claimed the territory of Judah. The Samaritans moved into the north; the Edomites moved into the south; the Philistines occupied land in the west; and the Ammonites threatened from the east. Judah was a small land, just a little part of one of the many provinces of Cyrus's mighty empire.

The returned exiles settled down, some in Jerusalem, but most in nearby towns and villages. After they had found new homes, they met together in Jerusalem. Joshua the high priest and Zerubbabel, nephew of Prince Sheshbazzar, led the people in rebuilding the altar of the Lord in front of the ruins of the temple.

As soon as the altar was finished, the people offered sacrifices to the Lord. After that day, they held regular morning and evening services at the altar.

The next project was rebuilding the temple. First they collected silver and gold to pay the masons and carpenters, and food supplies to send to Lebanon in exchange for cedar wood. By the end of their first year back, they were ready to begin.

They built the foundation of the new temple on the ruins of the old one, for this was a special place chosen by God. When the foundation was in place, they held a special worship service to celebrate. The priests dressed in their best robes and blew their trumpets to call the people to worship.

Everyone praised the Lord together, singing

> It is good to give thanks to the Lord,
> for he is good;
> and his love for Israel
>   is everlasting.

The young people shouted with joy, praising the Lord for bringing them back to Judah. At the same time, the older people began to cry, for they were thinking about the first temple. The sounds of joy and sadness mixed together, producing a great noise that could be heard a long way off.

9

Rebuilding the Temple

Ezra 4—6; Haggai

DURING the time of the exile, the people of God, who were known as Israelites, began to be called Jews, meaning people of Judah, even though many of them lived outside the land of Judah.

The Jews who returned to Judah found a mixed people called Samaritans living nearby. The Samaritans were descended from the ten tribes of the old Northern Kingdom of Israel and from foreigners who had come as captives of the Assyrians two hundred years before. The

Samaritans worshiped the Lord, but the Jews were suspicious of them.

When the Samaritans heard that some exiles had returned to rebuild the temple, they went to Joshua and Zerubbabel and the other leaders of the Jews in Jerusalem.

"Let us join you in building the temple," they said. "We've been worshiping your God ever since we came to this land."

"No," answered the Jewish leaders. "The temple we're building for our God is none of your business. We'll build it by ourselves, as Cyrus has ordered."

Then the Samaritans began to work against the Jews. They bribed the Persian officials to discourage the Jews from continuing their building project. The Jews were so afraid of the Samaritans and the Persians that they gave up their plans for rebuilding the temple.

This continued for the rest of the time that Cyrus was king, during the reign of Cyrus's son Cambyses, and on into the reign of Darius—for more than fifteen years.

During these years Judah suffered from bad weather. Little rain came down, so the crops couldn't grow, and the people and the animals didn't have enough food to eat.

In the late summer of the second year of the reign of Darius, the word of the Lord came to a prophet named Haggai, and Haggai spoke to the people of Judah.

"Hear the word of the Lord!" he said. "You say it's not time to rebuild the temple. Well, then, is it time for you to live in your nice new houses while the Lord's house lies in ruins? Think about what's been going on. You've been planting a lot of crops, but hardly anything grows. You don't have enough to eat and drink. You're so poor, you don't have enough clothes to wear. You can't support your families.

"Why are these things happening? Why does the Lord ruin your crops? Because the Lord's house is in ruins! That's why there has been no rain. The Lord himself has sent this drought.

"Now go up to the hills and gather timber. If you rebuild the temple, the Lord will bless you, and the glory of the Lord will be here among you."

Zerubbabel, prince of Judah, Joshua the high priest, and the people of Judah heard what Haggai said, and they were filled with fear.

Then Haggai encouraged them. "The Lord is with you," he said.

The Lord inspired the people to begin work. They gathered timber, prepared large blocks of stone, and organized the construction workers. In a few weeks, they were ready to rebuild the temple.

Then the Lord spoke to Haggai again, giving him another message for the people. "Go, speak to them," he said.

Haggai went to the Jews and said, "Is there

anyone here who remembers the splendor of the first temple, with its gold and silver? How does this building compare with it? Not much, is it? Well, don't be discouraged. Be strong, Zerubbabel. Be strong, Joshua. Be strong, all of you. Get to work, for the Lord is with you. Don't be afraid. All the silver and gold in the world belong to the Lord. The treasure of all the nations will come here to this temple, and the Lord will fill it with his glory. The glory of this temple will be even greater than the glory of the old temple!"

The people felt encouraged by Haggai's message, and they continued to work on the temple. They were making good progress until one day when some Persian officials came to Jerusalem to see what was going on.

"Who said you could rebuild this temple?" they demanded.

Tattenai, the Persian governor said, "Give us the names of the men who are responsible for this!"

The Jews answered, "We're the servants of the God of heaven and earth. We're rebuilding his temple. It was originally built by a great king of Israel. Our ancestors caused God to become angry, so he let their enemies conquer them and carry them into exile. Their enemies pulled down the temple and destroyed Jerusalem. But Cyrus ordered the temple to be rebuilt. He returned its equipment and let us come back here."

The Persian officials listened to this explanation, and then they sent a report to King Darius. God was watching over his people, for the officials let the Jews continue building the temple while they waited for the king's reply.

Finally, Darius sent his answer. He had discovered that it was true that Cyrus had ordered the temple to be rebuilt.

"Get out of Jerusalem!" Darius wrote to Governor Tattenai. "Let the Jews finish their temple. Help them with their expenses by paying them whatever they need from the royal treasury. Give them something for offerings, so their priests can make acceptable sacrifices to the God of heaven. Tell them to pray for God's blessing on me and my sons.

"If anyone disobeys this command," said

Darius, "punish him by pulling down his house and having him whipped. May the God of Jerusalem strike anyone who dares to disobey my order! I, Darius, have spoken."

Haggai's prophecy was beginning to come true. Silver and gold from the Persian treasury went to buy offerings for the temple of God.

10

The Holy City

Zechariah; Ezra 6

WHILE the Jews rebuilt the temple, Haggai and another prophet, a man named Zechariah, encouraged them with messages from the Lord.

Some of the people were confused about what the Lord required. They thought he would bless them for rebuilding the temple, no matter how they behaved. They thought he cared more about rules for fasting than about justice.

"Hear the word of the Lord!" cried Zechariah. "He wants you to be faithful. He wants you to be kind and to treat other people fairly. Return to the Lord, and he will return to you. Don't be like your ancestors, who ignored the Lord and his prophets. The Lord destroyed Jerusalem because your ancestors ignored the Lord's teachings."

Zechariah saw visions from the Lord, visions of a great Jerusalem, a strong and holy city. He saw Joshua the high priest and Zerubbabel prince of Judah ruling over God's people.

Zechariah wondered how God would cause these things to happen. How would Jerusalem become great?

"Not by military force," said the Lord. "Not by human power, but by my Spirit!"

In a vision Zechariah saw the Lord defeating

all the forces of evil, so his people could live in peace and safety. He saw a king from the family of David, a humble man who entered Jerusalem riding on a donkey.

Zechariah told the people that God wanted them to be holy. "The Lord hates lying, injustice, and violence," he said. Holiness meant treating other people kindly and fairly, and obeying the Lord's commandments.

He told the people about his vision of the future. All the nations of the world would come to the holy city of Jerusalem, and the Jews would be a blessing for all nations.

"The people of other nations will go to each other and say, 'Come, let us go look for the Lord,' and they will go to Jerusalem. Then the people of every race and language on earth will take a Jew by the sleeve and say, 'We want to go with you, for we have heard that God is with you.'

"The Lord won't leave you," said Zechariah. "He is your strength. You will be his people, and he will be your God."

Zechariah's words encouraged the Jews as they finished the temple. It took four and a half years to complete the building. Then the people held a great worship service to celebrate. They offered enormous sacrifices and sang praises to the Lord.

The temple was finished seventy years after it was destroyed. God's word through the prophet Jeremiah was coming true.

The Day of the Lord

Obadiah; Malachi; Joel

THE people of Judah were discouraged. For many years after the rebuilding of the temple, only a few families lived in Jerusalem. The city walls were still in ruins. Foreigners still controlled much of their territory. Under the Persian kings they had freedom to worship their God, but where was their own king? Where was the promised ruler from the family of David?

After the fall of Jerusalem the Edomites had been especially cruel. They had come up from the south to help the invaders rob and destroy

61

Jerusalem. Judah was still small and weak, while Edom was strong and powerful. It didn't seem right.

During the reign of Xerxes, son of Darius, a prophet named Obadiah brought the word of the Lord to the people of Judah. Obadiah spoke about a day of the Lord, a time in the future when God would punish the wicked and establish his justice over all the earth.

"The Lord will punish the Edomites!" said Obadiah. "He'll punish the leaders of that nation. He'll treat them as they have treated others. He'll restore to Israel all her lost territory. And some day the kingdom of God will cover the whole world!"

The people listened to Obadiah, but they still felt depressed. Sometimes they thought God didn't love them.

Then the Lord sent a prophet called Malachi to speak to them.

"God loves you," said Malachi. "See how he has treated you in the past; he has loved you more than he has loved the Edomites."

"Why doesn't the Lord answer our prayers?" asked the people.

"Because you don't keep your promises," answered Malachi. "Many of you have divorced your Jewish wives and married pagans. You know that's against God's commandments, because pagan wives will lead you to worship idols. You've broken the promises you made to the

women you married when you were young. They were your partners, and you have been disloyal to them. God hates divorce! He hates the cruel things you do to your wives."

Then the people complained that the Lord didn't punish evil and reward good. "Where is the God of justice?" they asked.

"Look," said Malachi. "Some day the Lord will send his messenger to prepare a path for him. Suddenly the Lord himself will come to his temple. And when that happens, no one will be able to stand it, for the Lord will punish the wicked."

Then Malachi said, "If you return to the Lord, he'll return to you."

"When did we turn away from him?" asked the people. "What have we done against him?"

"You break your promises," said Malachi. "You promised to give one tenth of your crops as an offering to the Lord. When you do, he'll bless you."

"It's no use serving God," complained the people. "What good does it do to obey him? We might as well act like wicked people. They disobey God all the time, and nothing ever happens to them. Look at them: they're happy and successful!"

"Listen," said Malachi. "The Lord watches over the people who honor him. He writes their names in his book. They belong to him, and he'll treat them like his children.

"One day in the future the wicked will be destroyed, and those who serve the Lord will be blessed.

"Before this great and terrible day of the Lord, he will send a prophet like Elijah. That prophet will cause parents and children to return to each other, so the land won't be destroyed."

Malachi encouraged the people to live according to God's teachings. He told the priests to offer pure sacrifices to the Lord. His messages helped the Jews know what God was like, and how he wanted them to live.

Another prophet who spoke to the people of Judah was Joel. Joel saw visions of locusts invading and destroying the land.

"Sound the alarm!" he cried. "Warn the people

of the danger! The Lord is sending great destruction. The day of the Lord is coming—a day of darkness and gloom, a day of cloud and dense fog. Locusts will come like soldiers on war horses, destroying everything in their way. Who will be able to stand it?"

Then Joel spoke messages of hope. "If you turn back to the Lord," he said, "the Lord will forgive you, for he is good. He's ready to bless everyone who calls on him. He'll have mercy on his people. He'll drive out the invaders and make up for the years that the locusts destroy."

In the future, said Joel, the Lord will bless his people in a new and wonderful way.

> The day will come
> > when I will pour out my Spirit
> > > on all people.

> Your sons and daughters
> > will prophesy,
> your old men
> > will dream dreams,
> and your young men
> > will see visions.

> I will pour out my Spirit
> > in those days
> > > even on the slaves,
> > > men and women.

"Everyone who calls on the name of the Lord will be saved," said Joel. "The Lord will judge all nations. He'll defend his people against their enemies. He'll bless Jerusalem and make it a holy city. It will be full of people forever, and the Lord will make his home here!"

Obadiah, Malachi, and Joel gave the people hope and helped them remember God's teachings. God was in control of history, they said. Even though Judah was poor and weak and Jerusalem was in ruins, the Lord God planned a great future for his people.

12

Nehemiah's Secret Plan

Ezra 4; Nehemiah 1—2

NEHEMIAH was a royal official who lived in Susa, the winter capital of the Persian kings. One day Nehemiah's brother Hanani arrived with some visitors from Judah.

"How is Jerusalem?" asked Nehemiah. "How are the Jews?"

"They're in great trouble and disgrace," answered the visitors. "The city walls are broken down. The gates of the city haven't been repaired since they were destroyed a hundred and forty years ago."

Hanani and the other visitors told Nehemiah how the Jews had been having problems with the Samaritans. At the beginning of the reign of Xerxes, the Samaritans had made written complaints against them. When Xerxes' son Artaxerxes became king, the Samaritans convinced the Persian officials to write to the king against the Jews. They said that if the Jews rebuilt Jerusalem, the city would be a threat to the empire. The Jews wouldn't pay their taxes; they would rebel against the king.

Artaxerxes ordered the Jews to stop rebuilding Jerusalem, for he was afraid that if they rebuilt the city and its walls, he would lose control of that part of his empire.

When he heard this news, Nehemiah felt so bad, he sat down and cried. For several days he mourned by fasting and praying.

"O Lord God of heaven," he prayed. "O great

and awesome God, you always keep your promises to those who honor you. Please listen to my prayer for your people. We sinned against you in the past, and you punished us. Then you forgave us and brought some of your people back to Judah. O Lord, please hear my prayer and the prayers of your people. Please inspire the king to be kind to me."

Nehemiah was thinking of a plan, a secret plan to help Jerusalem. He was the king's butler. It was his job to serve wine to the king at the royal table. One day soon after Hanani's visit, Nehemiah was serving wine to the king and queen and feeling very unhappy.

As the king took the wine from Nehemiah's hand, he said, "Why do you look so sad? You aren't sick. You must be depressed about something."

Nehemiah was afraid of the power of the king. (This was the same Artaxerxes who had ordered the Jews to stop rebuilding Jerusalem.) "May the king live forever!" he said. "How can I help looking sad when the city of my ancestors is in ruins and its gates have been burned down?"

"What do you want from me?" asked the king.

Nehemiah prayed silently to the Lord before he answered. "If the king is pleased with me," he said, "give me permission to go to Judah, to the city where my ancestors are buried, so I may rebuild the city."

"How long will the journey take?" asked the

king. "When will you return?"

Nehemiah answered the king's questions, and the king gave him permission to go to Judah.

"If it please the king," said Nehemiah, "give me letters for the governors of the province, ordering them to help me by giving me timber and other supplies."

The king gave Nehemiah everything he asked for because the gracious hand of the Lord was on Nehemiah. The king gave Nehemiah an escort of army officers and horsemen and letters for the Persian officials in Judah.

When Nehemiah arrived in Jerusalem, he didn't tell anyone his secret plan. He knew the enemies of the Jews would try to stop him if they found out what he wanted to do. He waited for three days, and then he took a few men and went out in the middle of the night. He didn't even tell the leaders of Judah what he was doing.

He left the city through the Valley Gate, riding a donkey. He circled around the ruins of the wall, south past Dragon's Fountain and the Dung Gate, inspecting the places where the wall had been broken down and the gates had been destroyed.

On the east side of the city he crossed over to the Fountain Gate and the King's Pool. Then he rode south until he came to a place that was too narrow for his donkey to pass through. He turned down into the Kidron Valley and inspected the wall on the east side of the city. He returned the same way, arriving back inside the city without anyone knowing where he had been and what he had been doing.

After his midnight inspection tour, Nehemiah completed his plan for helping Jerusalem. He went to the leaders of the Jews and told them what he wanted to do.

"You see the trouble we're in," he said. "Jerusalem lies in ruins, its gates destroyed by fire. Come, let's rebuild the walls of the city. Let's end this disgraceful situation!"

He told them how the Lord had been with him and how King Artaxerxes had helped him.

"Let's go," answered the leaders of the Jews. "Let's rebuild the walls of Jerusalem!"

13

Rebuilding the Walls of Jerusalem

Nehemiah 2—7, 12

WHEN the enemies of the Jews heard about Nehemiah's plan to rebuild the walls of Jerusalem, they were very angry. Sanballat, ruler of Samaria, went to see Nehemiah. With him he took Tobiah, ruler of Ammon, and Geshem, ruler of Edom.

"What do you think you're doing?" they asked. "Are you rebelling against the king?"

Nehemiah answered, "The God of heaven will give us success. We're God's servants, and you people have no claim to anything in this city!"

Nehemiah and the Jewish leaders encouraged the people to work with great energy. They organized them into groups of families, dividing the wall into forty sections. Each group repaired and rebuilt a section of the wall. Everyone helped, from the priests and merchants to the humblest peasants. Rich and poor, young and old joined together to lay beams, set doors in the gates, and repair the wall with the old stones that were lying in heaps of rubble.

As they worked, their enemies became angrier. They feared that the Jews would become powerful again.

Sanballat and Tobiah made fun of the Jews in front of the wealthy men of Samaria. "What do those pathetic Jews think they're doing?" asked Sanballat. "Do they think they can rebuild the city? Can they make building stones out of heaps of burnt rubble?" He pointed to the wall and laughed.

"Let them build," said Tobiah. "Whatever flimsy sort of wall they put up, a fox will knock down!"

Nehemiah overheard their comments, and he prayed, "O Lord, hear our prayer. Our enemies hate us. Make their rude remarks fall on their own heads. Make them suffer as we have suffered. Don't let them go unpunished!"

The Jews kept on working. They filled in the gaps and built the wall up to half its old height, for they were working with all their hearts.

When their enemies saw what progress the Jews were making, they said to each other, "Let's sneak up and attack them before they know what's happening. Let's strike them down and put an end to Nehemiah's plans."

Some Jews who lived near the Samaritans heard them plotting together, and they went and warned the workers. This happened so many times, the workers became discouraged.

"We feel weary," they said. "There's too much rubble to clear away. We'll never be able to rebuild the wall by ourselves."

"Don't be afraid," said Nehemiah. "The Lord is stronger than your enemies!"

He put armed guards behind the wall and passed out swords, spears, and bows to the workers. "Fight for your families," he told them. "Fight for your brothers, your sons and daughters, your wives, and your homes!"

Nehemiah divided the workers into two groups. Half of them continued to build the wall while the other half stood guard. Even the men who carried building materials kept one hand on their loads and one hand on their weapons. All the workers carried swords in their belts.

Nehemiah stationed a man with a trumpet up on the wall and said to the people, "We need an alarm system. The work is so spread out, we're too widely separated from each other. When you hear the sound of the trumpet, come here at once. Our God will fight for us!"

Then the Jews went back to work, half of them holding spears and standing guard against their enemies. They worked from the time the sun rose in the morning until the stars came out at night. They slept inside the city so their enemies couldn't sneak up on them in the dark. They slept in their clothes with their hands on their spears.

When their enemies realized they couldn't attack the Jews, they tried to trick Nehemiah. They sent him a message saying, "Come, meet us at the village in Ono Valley."

Nehemiah answered, "I have important work to do. I can't come down. Why should the work stop while I meet with you?"

Four times Sanballat, Tobiah, and Geshem sent the same message, and four times Nehemiah gave the same answer.

Next they wrote him a letter saying, "We hear that you Jews are planning to rebel against the government. That's why you're rebuilding the city walls. And you, Nehemiah, are planning to set yourself up as king of Judah. Well, we'll be sure that Artaxerxes hears about this! Now are you ready to come down and talk to us?"

"Nothing you say is true," answered Nehemiah. "You've made up the whole thing."

He knew they were trying to frighten him, so he worked even harder. "Strengthen my hand, O God!" he prayed.

In spite of all these problems, the Jews finished the wall in fifty-two days, and their enemies realized that the power of the Lord had helped them.

The Jews held a special worship service to dedicate the wall. Nehemiah asked the leaders of the people to come up to the top of the wall, where he divided them into two groups. One group walked one way around the wall while the other walked in the opposite direction. The singers, musicians, and priests followed the leaders. The two groups met near the entrance of the temple. There they praised the Lord with loud singing.

All the people on the ground looked up and shouted with joy. Their shouts made a great sound that could be heard a long way off.

14

Ezra Teaches the Torah

Ezra 7—10; Nehemiah 8—11, 13

NEHEMIAH stayed in Judah for twelve years, helping the people and encouraging them to obey God's commandments. He asked more families to move into Jerusalem, which still had few people. He settled problems between the rich people and the poor people. He told the rich to forgive the debts of the poor so they wouldn't have to sell their homes and become slaves.

Nehemiah set a good example. He didn't spend his government salary on himself, but shared it with others. He honored the Lord by treating the people kindly and fairly.

About this same time, the Lord sent another leader to Jerusalem to help the Jews. This was Ezra, a Jewish scribe who lived and taught in Babylon. Ezra studied the Torah, the teachings of God given in the law of Moses.

When Ezra heard about the problems of the Jews in Jerusalem and Judah, he asked the king for permission to go and investigate.

Artaxerxes gave Ezra everything he asked for, even ordering his officials in Judah to give Ezra anything else he needed. He gave him permission to teach the Torah to the people.

Ezra took the silver and gold that the king gave

him for the temple, and he prayed, "Praise the Lord, the God of our ancestors! He has inspired the king to add glory to the temple; he has caused the king and his officials to help me."

When Ezra asked the leaders of the Babylonian Jews to go with him, some agreed while others donated offerings for the temple in Jerusalem.

Ezra asked the people who agreed to go to fast and pray to the Lord for a safe journey. He was embarrassed to ask the king for a military escort, for he had told the king that the Lord would protect them on their journey.

The Lord answered their prayers. He kept them from thieves and other dangers and brought them safely to Judah.

After Ezra and his friends settled in their new homes, Ezra called the people together. Old settlers and new—men, women, and children—gathered in front of the temple.

Ezra opened the scroll of the Torah, and the people stood up.

"Praise the Lord, the great God!" he said.

"Amen, amen!" answered the people, raising their hands to heaven.

Then the people bowed down to worship the Lord, and Ezra read to them from the Torah. As he read, some other men explained the meaning of God's teachings.

All the people listened carefully, from early morning until the middle of the day. When they understood how God wanted them to live, they began to cry, for they realized that they had been disobeying the Lord's commandments.

"Don't be sad," said the men standing with Ezra. "This is a holy day, a day for celebrating and feasting. Eat rich food and drink sweet drinks. Share with the poor. But don't cry. The joy of the Lord will make you strong!"

Then the people went off to feast and celebrate, giving thanks to the Lord for teaching them through the Torah.

Then Ezra found out that the people were offending God. Many of them had pagan wives. Some of them didn't give their best offerings to the temple. Others broke the rules about resting on the Sabbath day.

Ezra taught the people to separate themselves from foreigners. They sent away their pagan wives and promised to obey God's commandments.

When Nehemiah returned to Jerusalem a few years later, he found some of the same problems. He encouraged the people to change their behavior, insisting that they live according to the Torah.

In these years after the exile, the Jews kept away from foreigners. They lived quietly in their own land, worshiping the Lord and following his teachings.

The Story of
Esther

15

Celebrating the Power of Persia

Esther 1

XERXES, king of Persia, was rich and powerful. He ruled over an empire that stretched from India to Ethiopia and included one hundred and twenty-seven provinces. He ruled over many nations, over people of many different races and languages.

In the third year of his reign Xerxes (who was also called Ahasuerus) gave a banquet at his winter palace in Susa to celebrate his power. He invited his high officials, his army commanders, his noblemen, and the governors of all the provinces. For six months they feasted while he showed off the wealth and magnificence of his court.

Then Xerxes invited the men of Susa, both rich and poor, to come to another banquet. This second party was held in the palace garden and lasted for a week.

The courtyard of the garden was richly decorated with royal purple curtains hanging from marble columns. The courtyard itself was paved with bright stones of red, blue, and white.

In this splendid garden Xerxes' guests reclined on gold and silver couches, eating and drinking wine from beautifully decorated golden cups. Each guest could drink as much as he wanted, for the king told his servants to pour them all the wine they asked for.

While the king and the men were drinking in the garden, Queen Vashti was giving a party for the women inside the palace.

By the evening of the seventh day of the banquet, the king was feeling good from all the wine he had been drinking. He called for his seven personal servants and told them to bring Queen Vashti to him, wearing her royal crown. The drunken king wanted to show off his beautiful queen in front of his guests.

When the king's servants went to fetch the queen, she refused to obey the king's command. This made the king so furious, he immediately sent for his seven chief advisers.

"What should I do?" he asked them. "What does the law say about a queen who refuses to obey the king's command?"

One of the advisers, a man named Memucan, answered, "Queen Vashti has done wrong—and not only to the king. She has insulted all the royal officials and every man in the empire! When the women hear about what she has done, they won't respect their husbands.

"If it please the king," he advised, "let him issue a royal decree saying that Vashti may never again appear before the king. Let the decree be written into the laws of the Medes and Persians, so it can never be changed. Then let the king give Vashti's place as queen to some other woman. When the women of the empire hear this decree, they will all show proper respect to their husbands!"

The king and his officials were pleased with Memucan's advice. He sent letters to all the provinces of the empire, to each nation in its own language, proclaiming that every man should be master in his own house.

16

A Royal Beauty Contest

Esther 2

SOME time later, when Xerxes' anger cooled down, he remembered Vashti and what she had done and what he had decided to do to her.

His advisers said to him, "Let the king order a beauty contest. Appoint officials in every province to find the most lovely maidens and bring them to Susa. Put them in the harem, where they can receive beauty treatments. Then take the girl who most pleases the king and make her queen in Vashti's place."

Xerxes thought this was a good idea, so he appointed officials to search the empire for beautiful young girls. They brought the girls to his palace and put them in the harem.

Among these girls was a Jewish orphan named Hadassah, who was also called Esther. When Esther's mother and father died, her cousin Mordecai had adopted her; he had brought her up as his own daughter. Mordecai was a member of the tribe of Benjamin. His family had been taken captive from Jerusalem by Nebuchadnezzar.

Esther was beautiful and graceful, with a pleasant personality. Hegai, the official in charge of the harem, liked her so much that he treated her better than all the other girls. He gave her everything she needed for her beauty treatment and sent seven maids from the palace to wait on her. He put Esther and her maids in the best part of the harem.

Esther didn't tell anyone that she was Jewish, because Mordecai had told her not to. Mordecai wasn't allowed to visit her, but every day he walked back and forth in front of the courtyard of the harem, to find out how Esther was doing and how she was being treated.

Esther and the other girls spent a year in the harem preparing to meet the king. They received beauty treatments of precious oils and perfumes, and they were given expensive clothes and jewelry. When it was each girl's turn to go to the king, she was allowed to wear whatever clothes and jewelry she wanted. Each girl went in to the king's apartment in the evening, and the next morning she moved to a different part of the palace, to the harem of the king's wives. No girl was allowed to return to see the king a second time unless he especially liked her and asked for her by name.

At last it was Esther's turn to go to the king. Hegai helped her choose clothes and jewelry. Everyone who knew Esther thought she was charming, and when she went to the king, he liked her more than any of the other maidens. He was so pleased with her, he placed the royal crown on her head and made her queen in Vashti's place.

Then the king gave a banquet in Esther's honor and invited all his important officials. He proclaimed a holiday throughout the empire and gave gifts to his subjects to celebrate Esther's coronation.

Even after Esther had won the king's favor, she continued to obey Mordecai. And she didn't tell anyone that she was Jewish.

17

Haman's Decree Against the Jews

Esther 2—4

NEAR the time that Esther became queen, Mordecai became an official at the royal court, working at the palace gate. One day while he was there, he found out that two of the king's servants, Bigthan and Teresh, were angry with the king and were plotting to assassinate him.

Mordecai told Esther, and Esther told the king. The king ordered an investigation. When he found out that Mordecai's report was true, he had the plotters executed by hanging them on a gallows.

Then the king ordered an account of these events written down in the official daily record of the empire. But he forgot to reward Mordecai.

Some time after this the king promoted a royal official named Haman. Haman was a descendant of the Amalekite king, Agag, an ancient enemy of the tribe of Benjamin (Mordecai's tribe). The king made Haman his prime minister and commanded all his other officials to bow down before him. All of them obeyed except Mordecai.

"Why do you disobey the king's command?" the other officials asked Mordecai. Every day they asked him why he refused to kneel or bow down to Haman, but he ignored them.

Finally the officials told Haman about Mordecai's behavior. They wondered what Haman would do, for Mordecai had told them that he was a Jew.

Haman was furious. And when he found out that Mordecai was a Jew, he made up his mind to destroy all the Jews in the empire.

At the beginning of the new year, in the twelfth year of the reign of Xerxes, Haman ordered some astrologers to cast lots to help him decide when to take his revenge on Mordecai. The lots, called "purim," fell on the thirteenth day of the twelfth month, almost a year away.

Haman went to see the king. "O king," he said. "There's a certain nation of people who are scattered among all the other nations in your empire. They're in every province, but they keep to themselves. They follow their own customs and obey their own laws. Since they don't obey the king's laws, it's not in the king's interest to tolerate them.

"Now, if it please the king," he said, "send out a decree ordering these people to be destroyed. I'll pay ten thousand talents of silver to the royal treasury if you do."

"Well," said the king, "if that's what you want to do, it's all right with me."

Then he took off his signet ring—the ring engraved with the royal seal—and gave it to Haman.

Haman sent for the royal secretaries and dictated a decree. He signed the order with the

king's name and sealed it with the king's seal.

Haman's decree ordered the people of the empire to kill all the Jews, men and boys, women and children, in one day—the thirteenth day of the twelfth month. He encouraged the enemies of the Jews to slaughter them without mercy and to take all their possessions.

The decree was first announced in Susa. Then messengers carried copies to all the provinces of the Persian Empire, from India to Ethiopia.

While Haman and the king sat down to feast and drink, the people of Susa were confused and upset.

When Mordecai found out what was happening, he tore his clothes and put on sackcloth and covered his head with ashes. He went out into the city, crying bitterly. He stopped at the palace gate, for people in mourning weren't allowed inside.

And all over the empire the king's messengers announced Haman's decree. When the Jews heard it, there was great mourning, with fasting, weeping, and wailing. Many of them put on sackcloth and ashes.

18

Esther Prepares a Banquet and Haman Prepares a Gallows

Esther 4—5

WHEN Esther's servants told her that Mordecai was outside the gate, dressed in sackcloth and ashes, she was so upset, she sent clothing out to him. He refused to put it on.

Then she sent her servant, Hathach, to find out what was happening.

Hathach found Mordecai in the city square in front of the palace. Mordecai told him about Haman's decree and gave him a copy of it to show to Esther. He told him to tell Esther to go to the king and beg for mercy for the Jews. Hathach gave Esther Mordecai's message. Then he went back to Mordecai with her answer.

"If any man or woman goes to the king in the inner courtyard without being invited, that person is put to death," said Esther. "It's the law, and everyone knows it. There's only one way to escape death. If the king holds out his golden scepter to the person who goes to him, then that person's life is spared. But," she added, "the king hasn't invited me to see him for thirty days!"

Mordecai answered, "Don't think that you'll be any safer than the other Jews just because you live in the palace. If you remain silent at a time like this, help will come from some place else. The Jews will be saved, but you and your father's family will perish. Who knows? Perhaps you came to the throne for just such a time as this!"

"All right," said Esther. "Go, tell all the Jews in Susa to fast for me. Tell them not to eat or drink for three days and three nights. My maids and I will keep the same fast. Then I'll go to the king, even though it's against the law. If I perish, I perish!"

Mordecai did as Esther said, and all the Jews in Susa fasted for three days and three nights. Esther and her maids kept the same fast. They did this so God would hear their prayers for help.

On the third day Esther put on her royal robes and went to see the king. She stood in the inner courtyard, facing the throne room where he was sitting.

When the king noticed Esther standing there, he held out his golden scepter. She went up to him and touched the tip of it.

"What do you want, Queen Esther?" asked the king. "What's your request? You may have whatever you ask for, even if it's half my kingdom!"

"If it please the king," answered Esther, "let him come with Haman today to a banquet that I have prepared."

The king turned to his servants and said, "Tell Haman to come at once so we may do as Esther says."

The king went with Haman to Esther's banquet, and while they were drinking their wine, he said to her, "What's your request? What do you want? You may have whatever you ask for, even if it's half my kingdom!"

Esther answered, "What do I want? What do I request? If the king will give me what I want and do as I ask—if he is pleased with me—then come with Haman tomorrow to another banquet that I will prepare. Tomorrow I will tell you what I want."

Haman left the palace in high spirits, feeling very pleased with himself. On his way out he saw Mordecai at the gate. When Mordecai didn't stand up or show any sign of respect, Haman was filled with rage. But he kept control of himself and went on home.

As soon as he arrived at his house, Haman sent for his friends. He bragged to them and to his wife, Zeresh, about how much property he owned, about the ten sons he had, and about how the king had promoted him.

"That's not all," said Haman. "Today Queen Esther invited me, and only me, to go with the king to a banquet she had prepared. Then she invited us to go again tomorrow to another banquet."

Then his expression changed and he said, "But as long as I see Mordecai the Jew sitting at the palace gate, none of these things satisfy me."

Haman's wife and friends gave him some advice. "Have a gallows built," they said. "Make it seventy-five feet high. And early tomorrow morning go to the king and ask him to have Mordecai hanged on the gallows. Then you'll be able to enjoy Esther's banquet!"

Haman liked their suggestion so much, he prepared the gallows.

19

A Royal Reward

Esther 6

THAT night the king couldn't get to sleep, so he ordered his servants to bring the daily record book and read to him from it. They happened to read the account of how Mordecai had saved the king from being assassinated.

"What great honor did we give to Mordecai?" asked the king.

"Nothing," answered his servants.

"Let me see," said the king. "Who's in the palace now? Have any of my officials arrived yet?"

It was still quite early, but Haman had just entered the courtyard. He had hurried to the palace to ask the king to have Mordecai hanged on the gallows.

"Haman's outside, waiting to see you," said the king's servants.

"Send him in."

When Haman came in, the king said, "Tell me, what should I do for a man I especially want to honor?"

Haman said to himself, "Who else could that be but me!" Then he said to the king, "If the king wants to honor someone, have royal robes brought for him—robes the king himself has

101

worn. Have a crown put on the king's horse, and have one of the king's highest officials dress the man in the robes, mount him on the horse, and lead him through the city square. Have the official call out, 'See how the king rewards the man he especially wants to honor!' "

"Hurry!" said the king. "Go and get the robes and the horse and do just as you have suggested. Do all these things for Mordecai the Jew. You'll find him sitting at the palace gate. Don't forget a single thing!"

Haman took the royal robes and the king's horse and did as the king commanded. He put the robes on Mordecai and led him on horseback through the city square, calling out to the people, "See how the king rewards the man he especially wants to honor!"

Then Mordecai went back to his place at the palace gate, and Haman hurried home, covering his face in shame.

He told his wife and friends what had just happened.

"Because of Mordecai," they said, "you're beginning to fall. And since he's a Jew, you will never again rise above him. In fact, because of him, you will fall again."

While they were still talking, the king's servants arrived in a hurry to escort Haman back to the palace for Esther's second banquet.

Mordecai's Decree for the Jews

Esther 7—8

WHAT do you want, Queen Esther?" asked the king. He was drinking wine with Haman at Esther's banquet. "I'll give you whatever you want," he promised. "Even if it's half my kingdom, I'll do it!"

"If it please the king," answered Esther, "I ask for my life. That's what I want. And the lives of my people. That's what I ask. For my people and I have been sold for slaughter. If we'd just been sold into slavery, I'd remain silent. I wouldn't bother you about it. But my people are about to be destroyed! Wiped out! Exterminated!"

"Who's responsible for this?" shouted the king. "Where is he? Who dares to plot such evil?"

"An enemy!" cried Esther. "A persecutor! This wicked Haman here!"

Haman was so shocked, he couldn't say a word. The king stood up in a rage and went out to the garden. Haman realized that the king had made up his mind to punish him, so he threw himself on Esther's couch, begging her for mercy.

A moment later the king returned and found Haman on the couch.

"What's going on here?" he roared. "Is this man actually going to attack my queen in my own house?"

As soon as the king said this, the palace servants covered Haman's head, for he was a man condemned to death.

Then a servant named Harbona spoke up. "Haman has built a gallows at his house," he said. "He was planning to hang Mordecai, the man who saved the king's life. The gallows is seventy-five feet high."

"Hang Haman on it!" commanded the king.

Haman died on the gallows he had prepared for Mordecai. Then the king's anger cooled down.

According to the law, a criminal's belongings became the property of the king, so that same day Xerxes took all of Haman's property and gave it to Queen Esther. When Esther told him that Mordecai was related to her, the king sent for him and gave him his royal signet ring. He promoted Mordecai to prime minister, in Haman's place. Then Esther gave Mordecai all of Haman's property.

Then Esther went in to see the king. She threw herself at his feet, crying and begging him to stop Haman's plot against the Jews.

The king held out his golden scepter, and Esther stood up.

"If it please the king," she said, "if you approve my request—if you really care about me—please issue an order to stop Haman's plans. He has arranged for the destruction of all the Jews in your

empire. How can I stand to see this disaster strike my own people? How can I bear to watch the destruction of my relatives?"

Xerxes answered, "I have done what I can. I've had Haman hanged, and I've given you his property. But I can't change a decree written in my name and sealed with the royal seal. It is the law. But you have my permission to write to the Jews in my name and to use the royal seal. Do whatever you think best."

The king sent for the royal secretaries, and Mordecai dictated a decree. He signed the decree with the king's name and sealed it with the king's seal.

Mordecai's decree said that the king would let the Jews defend themselves against their enemies. They could fight anyone who attacked them, and take all their possessions.

The decree was first announced in Susa; then messengers on strong, fast horses carried copies to all the provinces of the empire, from India to Ethiopia.

This new decree went into effect on the thirteenth day of the twelfth month—the exact same day that Haman had ordered the slaughter of the Jews.

The people of Susa filled the city with shouts of joy. Mordecai dressed himself in a royal robe and a cloak of fine linen and purple and covered his head with a great golden turban. Then he left the palace and went out into the city.

All over the empire the king's messengers announced the news of the decree. When the Jews heard it, there was great celebration, with feasting and shouts of joy.

21

Celebrating the Power of God

Esther 9—10

MORDECAI, prime minister of Persia, was so powerful, even the king's officials were afraid of him. Because of Mordecai's position, the people of the empire were afraid to hurt the Jews. On the thirteenth day of the twelfth month, many of them stood with the Jews against their enemies. The Jews defended themselves and killed the people who attacked them. But they didn't take anyone's property.

In Susa the Jews killed five hundred of their enemies, including the ten sons of Haman.

Xerxes reported this to Esther. "If the Jews have killed that many men in Susa," he said, "imagine what they're doing in the provinces. Now tell me, is there anything else I can do for you? You may have whatever you ask. Just tell me, and it will be yours."

"If it please the king," said Esther, "let the Jews in Susa have one more day to defend themselves. And hang the bodies of Haman's sons from the gallows."

The king did as Esther said.

Mordecai wrote an account of everything that happened, and then he sent letters to the Jews in all the provinces of the empire. He told them to

celebrate the fourteenth and fifteenth days of the twelfth month as a holiday every year, so they would never forget how their sorrow was changed to joy and how their mourning was changed to gladness. He told them to celebrate these days with feasts and parties, to exchange gifts, and to give presents to the poor.

Every year after that the Jews celebrated, calling the holiday Purim, from the word for lots, because Haman had cast lots to destroy them. Every Jewish family of every generation in every land celebrated the days of Purim, remembering how their sorrow was changed to joy and their mourning was changed to gladness.

Queen Esther made Mordecai's letters official by signing a decree. By her royal command Purim was celebrated all over the empire.

Xerxes continued to reign over his empire with great success. He filled his treasury with gold and silver from the taxes of every province of the empire.

Mordecai was popular with the Jews, who respected him highly, for he saw that they were treated well, and he looked after all their needs.

Struggling with God

A Storm at Sea

Jonah 1—2

GOD loved his people and did wonderful things for them. When they mourned, he comforted them. When they were in danger, he saved them from their enemies.

God also cared about the people of other nations, even the most wicked, for he was full of goodness and mercy.

One day the Lord said to the prophet Jonah, "Get up and go to the great city of Nineveh and preach against it. Tell the people of Nineveh that I have seen all their crimes."

Jonah got up and went—in the opposite direction. He went down to the port of Joppa, where he found a ship that was sailing to Tarshish, a port in the land of Spain, far to the west. Jonah paid his fare and went on board with the crew, for he wanted to escape from the Lord.

Then the Lord struck the ship with a violent storm. The wind blew so hard, the ship was in danger of falling apart.

The frightened sailors prayed for help, each to his own god. They they threw the cargo overboard to lighten the ship.

While this was going on, Jonah lay asleep in the bottom of the ship.

"Why are you sleeping so soundly?" asked the captain when he found Jonah. "Get up and pray

to your God for help. Maybe your God will answer and save us from death."

Up on the deck the sailors were saying to each other, "Come on, let's cast lots to find out if someone on this ship is causing our trouble!"

They cast lots, and the lot fell to Jonah.

"Now, then," they said, "what are you doing here? Where do you come from? What people do you belong to?"

"I'm a Hebrew," answered Jonah. "I worship the Lord, the God of heaven, who made the land and the sea." He told them he was trying to run away from the Lord.

The sailors were terrified to hear that Jonah was disobeying the Lord. And while they were talking, the storm was growing worse.

"What should we do to stop this storm?" they asked Jonah. They knew that the Lord had sent the storm.

"Take me and throw me into the sea," answered Jonah. "Then the wind will stop blowing and the sea will grow calm. I know it's my fault that this great storm has struck you."

The sailors tried to take the ship back to port. They rowed as hard as they could, but it was no use. The wind was blowing harder and harder.

Finally they cried out to the Lord. "O Lord," they said, "don't punish us for throwing this man overboard. You're responsible, we're not."

Then they picked Jonah up and threw him into the sea. Immediately, the wind stopped blowing and the sea grew calm.

When this happened, the sailors were so filled with the fear of the Lord, they offered sacrifices to him and promised to serve him.

The Mercy of God

Jonah 2—4

THE Lord caused a great fish to swallow Jonah. For three days and three nights Jonah stayed inside the belly of the fish.

From deep inside the fish he prayed to the Lord his God for help. "I'm not like the wicked people who worship other gods," he boasted. "Here I am, Lord, praying to you! I don't want to die. O Lord, save me, I will make a sacrifice to you. I promise. You are the one who saves."

The Lord spoke to the fish, and it spit Jonah out onto the seashore.

"Get up and go to the great city of Nineveh and preach to the people," said the Lord. "Give them the message I tell you."

This time Jonah got up and went to Nineveh. He walked across the city for a whole day. Nineveh was so large, it would have taken him three days to cross it.

Jonah preached to the people of Nineveh, giving them the Lord's message. "In forty days Nineveh will be turned upside down!" he cried.

The people of Nineveh listened to the word of the Lord. They felt so sorry for their sins, they stopped eating and began to fast. All the people, from the richest to the poorest, went without food. They wore sackcloth to show that they were sincerely sorry for their sins.

When the king of Nineveh heard what was go-

ing on, he got up from his throne and took off his royal robe. He put on sackcloth like everyone else and he humbly sat down in ashes as a sign of deep sorrow.

Then the king sent a proclamation to the people of Nineveh, saying, "Here is an order from the king and his officials. Nobody is to eat a thing. Everyone—even the cattle and the sheep— must not taste food or drink water. Everyone— even the animals—must wear sackcloth. Every-one must pray to God with all their might. Let everyone give up their wicked ways and turn from their evil habits. Perhaps God will change his mind and stop being angry with us. Perhaps he will let us live!"

God saw what they were doing and how sorry they were for their sins. When he noticed that the people of Nineveh were giving up their wicked ways, he changed his mind and didn't punish them as he had threatened to do.

Jonah was unhappy and angry. "O Lord," he prayed. "I knew it. I knew you would do something like this! That's why I tried to run away from you. I knew you would forgive Nineveh, for you are full of goodness and mercy. I knew you are slow to anger, faithful and loving, and always ready to forgive. I can't stand it! Let me die. I don't want to go on living."

"What right do you have to be angry?" asked the Lord.

Then Jonah went out to a place east of the city,

where he sat down on the ground. He made a shelter for himself so he could sit in the shade and wait to see what would happen to Nineveh.

The Lord caused a small plant to grow up beside Jonah, giving him more shade and making him comfortable. Jonah was delighted with the plant.

But at dawn the next day God caused a worm to attack the little plant, and it withered and died. Later that day, when the sun rose, God sent a hot east wind to blow on Jonah, and he caused the sun to beat down hard on his head.

Jonah was so hot, he thought he would faint. "I might as well be dead!" he prayed.

"What right do you have to be angry about the plant?" asked the Lord.

"I have every right to be angry," answered Jonah. "I'm so angry, I want to die!"

"You're upset about a little plant," said the Lord, "but you didn't take care of it or do anything to make it grow. The plant grew up and withered away overnight. Now tell me, shouldn't I feel sorry for the great city of Nineveh, with a hundred and twenty thousand innocent children and countless animals?"

24

What Happened to Job

Job 1—2

T HERE was once a man named Job. He lived a good life; he honored God, and he was careful to stay away from evil.

Job had seven sons and three daughters. He owned seven thousand sheep, three thousand camels, five hundred pairs of oxen, and five hundred donkeys. He also had a large number of servants. Job was the richest man in the East.

Job's sons used to take turns having banquets in their houses, one after the other. They invited each other and their three sisters to eat and drink with them. After each series of seven parties, Job would rise early in the morning and offer a sacrifice for each of his children.

"Perhaps," he said to himself, "one of them has sinned or accidentally offended God."

One day the members of the court of heaven appeared before the Lord. Satan, the accuser, was with them.

"Where have you been?" the Lord asked Satan.

"Roaming the earth," he answered. "Spying."

"Did you notice my servant Job?" asked the Lord. "There's nobody on earth as good and as faithful as Job. He honors me and he's careful to stay away from evil."

"Would Job honor you if you didn't reward him?" asked Satan. "You've protected him and his family and everything he owns. You've blessed everything he does. You've given him enough cattle to fill the land. Suppose you struck Job's property with disaster. If you took everything away from him, I bet he'd curse you to your face."

"All right," answered the Lord. "Everything he has is in your power. But keep your hands off Job himself."

Then Satan left the Lord's presence.

One day after this a messenger came running up to Job. "We were plowing the fields with the oxen," he said, "and the donkeys were grazing nearby. Suddenly some desert raiders swooped down from the south and carried off all the animals. They killed your herdsmen with their swords. I'm the only one to survive to tell the tale."

While the man was still speaking, another messenger arrived. "The fire of God flashed from heaven!" he cried. "It struck all your sheep and the shepherds and killed them. I'm the only one to survive to tell the tale."

While the second messenger was speaking, another man arrived. "Three bands of raiders came from the north!" he cried. "They took your camels, and they killed all the camel drivers with their swords. I'm the only one to survive to tell the tale."

While he was speaking, a fourth messenger arrived. "Your sons and daughters were eating and

drinking in their oldest brother's house," he said, "when suddenly a violent wind blew in from the desert. It knocked down the house, which fell down and killed all your children. I'm the only one to survive to tell the tale."

Job stood up and tore his clothes in grief. He shaved his head as a sign of mourning. Then he fell down to the ground and said, "I came into the world with nothing; I will leave the world with nothing. The Lord gives and the Lord takes away. Blessed be the name of the Lord!"

Job didn't sin or blame God for his troubles.

Then the members of the court of heaven appeared again before the Lord. Again, Satan was with them.

"Where have you been?" the Lord asked Satan.

"Roaming around the earth," he answered. "Spying."

"Did you notice my servant Job?" asked the Lord. "There's nobody on earth as good and as faithful as Job. He honors me and is careful to stay away from evil. In spite of all the disasters that have struck him, he hasn't sinned. You encouraged me to let you ruin him for no reason. Job is as faithful as ever."

Satan answered, "A man will give everything he has in order to stay alive. Suppose you struck his body with disease. If you did, I bet he'd curse you to your face."

"All right," answered the Lord. "He's in your power. But spare his life."

Then Satan left the Lord's presence.

Soon after this Satan struck Job with oozing sores from the top of his head to the bottom of his feet. Job was so miserable, he went and sat on top of an ash heap and scratched himself with a piece of a broken pot.

"Are you still faithful?" asked Job's wife. "Why don't you curse God and die?"

"You're talking like a foolish woman," answered Job. "If I accept the good things that God sends, how can I complain when he sends sorrow?"

Job didn't sin or blame God for his troubles.

Then Job's three friends, Eliphaz, Bildad, and Zophar, came to comfort him. They didn't recognize him at first, he looked so awful. They cried out loud and tore their clothing and threw dust over their heads. They went and sat down on the ground beside Job, staying there for seven days and seven nights without saying a word.

25

Job's Friends Try to Comfort Him

Job 4—37

"CURSE the day that I was born!" cried Job. "May that day be darkness! I wish that I had never lived, or died when I was a baby. Everything I feared has happened to me. My troubles are more than I can stand."

"May I speak?" asked Eliphaz. "You used to help other people when they were in trouble. Now let me help you. I have some advice. Everyone knows that God rewards goodness and punishes wickedness. That's what the wise men teach us. All of us have sinned, so all of us must be punished. If I were you, Job, I'd pray to God right now and confess my sins. If you do, God will heal you. Listen to me, Job! I know what I'm talking about."

"Your advice doesn't do me any good," answered Job. "What you say is stupid. I don't deserve this punishment. What terrible things have I done?"

"No, Job!" said Bildad. "God always rewards people who do right, and he always punishes sinners. Obviously, if you haven't sinned, then your children have. That's the answer! That's why you're being punished. Now go on and pray to God. If you're innocent, he'll reward you."

"I know I'm right," said Job. "But I'm so miserable, I'll soon die and go down to Sheol, the land of the dead. Until that happens, I'm going to keep on complaining. I won't be quiet, for God is attacking me! I know I can't win an argument with God. He's too powerful. I just wish someone would come between me and him. I know there must be someone who could redeem me. If not now, then after I die. Then I'll see God!"

"Be quiet, Job," said Zophar. "Don't talk like that! You say you're innocent, but it's not possible. If you're innocent, then God has to reward you. Everyone knows that. God blesses innocent people and punishes the guilty. And if you're being punished—well, you must be a sinner!"

Job's three friends kept telling him he deserved to be punished. Job kept saying he was innocent.

The more he complained, the more they were sure he was a wicked man. They thought he was attacking religion by questioning God.

"Stop it!" cried Job. "You criticize me for crying out to God, but you defend him with lies. Let him do what he wants with me—let him kill me. I'm innocent. I just wish I could prove it."

Day after day Job and his friends kept on arguing. Many people came to look at Job as he sat there on the ash heap, complaining to God. His skin was covered with disgusting, oozing sores. He was in constant pain. He was so thin, his bones stuck out.

The rich, healthy people were horrified to see what had happened to Job. The beggars and outcasts sneered at him. Nobody respected him. Nobody offered him any sympathy.

Job complained that life wasn't fair. Innocent people suffered while the wicked lived long and successful lives.

"I don't understand," he said. "I'm not guilty of any serious sin. I helped the poor. I wasn't proud. I gave hospitality to strangers. I admitted my faults. I didn't trust in riches. I didn't worship idols. I wasn't glad when my enemies suffered. I was kind to everyone. Oh, I was so happy in the old days! Everyone respected me then. Now they all laugh at me. I wish I could go back to the way things used to be."

The more Job complained, the more his friends were sure he was a terrible sinner. Finally,

Eliphaz, Bildad, and Zophar gave up on Job.

Then a young man named Elihu spoke to him. "I have wisdom from God," he said. "I may be young, but I know what I'm talking about."

Elihu told Job to consider God's great, mysterious power. God sends suffering to teach us lessons and to keep us from sinning, said Elihu. "God gives everyone what he deserves, Job. The wise men of Israel have taught us these things. You don't know what you're talking about. You're a a rebel. You can't understand God."

But Job kept complaining. "I won't be quiet," he said. "I'm innocent! I call on you, God, but you never answer. I want justice. Accuse me. Let me defend myself!"

26

The Voice from the Whirlwind

Job 38—42

A GREAT storm blew toward Job, and he heard a voice speaking to him from out of the whirlwind. It was the voice of the Lord God.

"Who are you to question me?" asked the voice. "Your words are empty and ignorant. Stand up like a man! I'll ask the questions and you'll answer.

"Where were you when I created the earth? Tell me, if you know so much, who decided on its measurements? Do you know? Who laid its foundations? Where were you then, Job?"

God asked Job about the sea and the sky, about the snow and the hail, the lightning, the stars, the clouds, and the mist.

"Do you understand how the wild animals live, Job? Tell me about lions and mountain goats, wild donkeys and buffaloes, ostriches, wild horses, and hawks. I watch over all of them.

"Well, Job, do you give up? Does the critic of Almighty God have an answer?"

"My words have been puny," said Job. "How can I answer? I put my hand over my mouth. I won't say anything else. I've already said more than I should."

Again the Lord spoke from the whirlwind, saying, "Now stand up like a man! I'll ask the questions and you'll answer. You accuse me of injustice in order to prove your own innocence. You don't have the power of God, Job. You don't have power over the earth, power over living creatures, power over the forces of evil."

Job said, "I know that you are powerful. You can do whatever you wish. I've spoken about things I didn't understand. Then I knew you only from hearing what other people said about you. But now I have seen you with my own eyes. I'm sorry. I take back everything I have said."

Then the Lord turned to Job's friends and said, "I'm angry with you, for you didn't tell the truth about me, as my servant Job has done. Take seven bulls and seven rams and give them to Job to offer as a sacrifice. Job will pray for you, and

I'll listen to his prayers and forgive you."

Eliphaz, Bildad, and Zophar did as the Lord commanded, and the Lord answered Job's prayer.

Then the Lord restored Job's fortunes and doubled his property.

Job's brothers and sisters and all his old friends came to visit him, and they feasted with him in his house. They gave him sympathy for all the troubles that the Lord had sent to him, and each of them gave him a silver coin and a gold ring.

The Lord blessed the end of Job's life more

than the beginning. He gave Job fourteen thousand sheep, six thousand camels, a thousand pairs of oxen, and a thousand donkeys.

He gave Job seven sons and three daughters. Job named the oldest daughter Jemimah, the middle one Keziah, and the youngest Keren-Happach. Job's daughters were the most beautiful women in the land. He gave them a full share of the inheritance, just like their brothers.

Job lived long enough to see his grandchildren and his great-grandchildren. He died content at the ripe old age of a hundred and forty.

27

A Time for Everything

Ecclesiastes

JOB had so much trouble, he questioned God about his suffering. Another person, called Ecclesiastes (the Teacher), had everything he wanted. Ecclesiastes questioned God about the meaning of life.

Ecclesiastes studied the wisdom of the Hebrews. He tested the sayings of the wise men to see if they were true. He could see that goodness isn't always rewarded and wickedness isn't always punished.

It seemed to Ecclesiastes that life is useless,

for everything ends in death. In those days the Jews didn't believe in an afterlife. They believed that everyone, good and bad, went to the underground world of the dead, called Sheol.

Ecclesiastes realized that no one can control his own life. Everyone depends on God—even the people who don't recognize God's power. So why bother? What's the use?

"Emptiness! Uselessness!" said Ecclesiastes. "What good does it do to work hard all your life? There's no profit in it. You die anyway.

"One generation goes and another comes after it, but the earth remains the same. The sun rises and the sun goes down; then it returns and begins all over again. The wind blows south, the wind blows north. Around and around it goes. Then it goes back and begins all over. All the rivers flow into the sea, but the sea is never filled. The water returns, and it starts all over again.

"Everything makes me tired. There's nothing new under the sun.

"I've studied everything, I've seen everything," said Ecclesiastes. "It's all useless, like chasing the wind.

"I did everything I could to be happy, but that was useless, too. I became rich. I built great mansions and I planted beautiful gardens. I had servants and animals, many possessions, silver and gold. I bought everything I wanted.

"But when I thought about it, I realized that it was all useless, like chasing the wind. It didn't mean a thing. "Certainly, wisdom is better than foolishness. But death ends everything, so what's the use?

"I became depressed, for everything I did amounted to nothing. I was depressed about my work and my possessions, for when I die, I can't take them with me.

"I realized that the best I can do is to enjoy life now. Eat, drink, enjoy what you've earned. This comes from God.

"I've noticed that God gives us work to do and a time for everything. There's a time for everything under the sun, a time that God chooses:

a time to be born and a time to die,
a time to wreck and a time to build,
a time to cry and a time to laugh,
a time to rip and a time to mend,
a time to be quiet and a time to talk,
a time to love and a time to hate,
a time for war and a time for peace.

"Everything is a gift from God," said Ecclesiastes. "When the time is right, he'll judge us all. Meanwhile, we live and die. The best we can do is to be happy in this life. Enjoy life as God gives it.

"We can't control what happens, no matter how rich or wise we may be. Nothing in this life lasts—not wealth, not fame, not even wisdom. The meaning of life is a mystery that only God knows. I've tried to figure it out, but it's beyond me.

"So I enjoy life as it comes. Life passes quickly and soon we grow old. We have only what God chooses to give us. And that's enough. It's no use worrying. The good in life is in living it. The profit of work is in doing it. The use of wisdom is in realizing how much we don't know."

Stories About Daniel

28

Daniel Obeys the Lord

Daniel 1

THE Chaldeans of Babylon were expert astrologers and fortune tellers. They observed the stars and planets; they recorded eclipses of the sun and the moon. They were famous for their ability to interpret dreams, to understand mysteries, and to tell the future.

In Babylon from the time of Nebuchadnezzar to the time of Cyrus there lived a wise man named Daniel. Daniel had been brought from Judah as a captive when the Lord handed Jerusalem over to Nebuchadnezzar.

Nebuchadnezzar placed the treasures of the temple of the Lord in the temple of his god. Then he ordered the head of his palace servants, a man named Ashpenaz, to select some boys from the Jewish captives, to train them for service at the royal court. He wanted young men from noble families who were handsome, intelligent, healthy, and well-educated. He told Ashpenaz to teach them the language and literature of the Chaldeans.

Every day the boys were given the same food and wine as the king and the other people at court. After three years of training they were expected to enter the king's service.

Among the boys who were chosen for this training were Daniel, Hananiah, Mishael, and Azariah. Ashpenaz gave them new names, calling them Belteshazzar, Shadrach, Meshach, and Abednego.

Daniel made up his mind to obey the strict Jewish rules about not eating certain foods. He asked Ashpenaz to help him, and God caused Ashpenaz to treat him kindly.

"I'm afraid of my lord the king," said Ashpenaz. "If you don't eat the food and wine the king has decided to give you, and then you don't look as healthy as the other boys, the king will kill me!"

Daniel went to the guard who was in charge of the boys. "Test us for ten days," he said. "Give us only vegetables to eat and water to drink. Then compare us with the boys who eat the king's food. If we look as healthy as they do, then treat us as we want."

The guard agreed to do what Daniel asked. When the ten days were up, Daniel and his friends looked healthier and stronger than any of the boys who had been eating the king's food.

After that, the guard let them have vegetables and water instead of the food and wine they were supposed to have.

God gave the four young men knowledge and understanding of all literature and science. In addition, he gave Daniel the ability to interpret all kinds of visions and dreams.

At the end of the three-year training period, Ashpenaz took all the boys to meet the king. As Nebuchadnezzar talked with them, he was most impressed with Daniel, Hananiah, Mishael, and Azariah.

The four young men entered the king's service. Whenever he needed wisdom and understanding, he found that they knew ten times more than all the magicians and enchanters in the whole kingdom.

29

Nebuchadnezzar's Dream

Daniel 2

ONE day Nebuchadnezzar called for his magicians, his enchanters, his sorcerers, and his astrologers. When they arrived, he said to them, "I have had a dream, and I'm upset about it. I must find out what it means."

"O king, live forever!" said the Chaldean wise men. "Tell us your dream, and we'll reveal the meaning to you."

"No," answerered the king. "I've decided that you must tell me what I have dreamed; then reveal what it means. If you can't tell me the

145

dream, I'll have you torn to pieces, and I'll have your houses torn down. But if you tell me, I'll give you rich gifts and great honors. Come on, tell me the dream and what it means."

"O king!" said the wise men. "If you will tell us the dream, we'll explain the meaning."

"Aha!" said the king. "You're stalling! You're afraid of being punished. I can tell that you've decided among yourselves to tell me some lies. Well, I'll believe your interpretation after you tell me the dream!"

"No one in the world can tell the king what he wants to know," said the wise men. "No king, not even the greatest and most powerful, has ever demanded such a thing from his wise men. What the king asks for is so difficult, only the gods could do it!"

Then Nebuchadnezzar flew into a rage, and he ordered all of the wise men of Babylon to be put to death.

When Daniel heard what was going on, he told his friends to pray to God for mercy, to ask him to reveal to them the mystery of the dream, so they and the other wise men of Babylon wouldn't be killed.

That night in a vision God revealed the secret to Daniel.

"May the name of God be blessed forever and ever," said Daniel. "He controls the time and the seasons. He sets up and brings down kings. He's the one who gives all wisdom and knowledge. He

reveals all mysteries; he knows every secret.

"I thank you, God of my ancestors, for answering my prayer and for showing me the meaning of the king's dream."

Then Daniel went to Arioch, the commander of the royal executioners. "Don't kill the wise men," he said. "Take me to see the king, and I'll reveal to him the meaning of his dream."

Arioch took Daniel to the king immediately. "O king," he said, "I've found a man among the Jewish exiles who can explain the meaning of the king's dream."

"Can you really tell me what I dreamed and what it means?" said the king to Daniel.

Daniel answered, "No man can solve the mystery of the king's dream. But there is a God in heaven who reveals secrets. He has shown the king what is going to happen in the future. And he has revealed to me the meaning of the dream. He didn't tell me because I'm wiser than anyone else, but so that the king will understand the meaning of his dream.

"In your dream, O king, you saw a giant metal statue standing in front of you. It was bright and shiny and terrifying to behold. The head of the statue was made of pure gold; its chest and arms were made of silver; its stomach and hips were bronze; its legs were iron; and its feet were part iron and part clay.

"While you were looking at the statue, a great stone broke loose from the side of the mountain. No human hands touched it or made it move. The stone struck the clay feet of the statue, shattering them. The whole statue crumbled into small pieces like fine powder, and the wind blew it away, leaving no trace.

"The stone that struck the statue grew into a mountain so huge that it covered the earth.

"That was your dream. Now I'll tell you what it means.

"You, O king, are the greatest of kings. The God of heaven has given you power and honor. He has made you ruler of a great kingdom, with power over people and animals. The golden head of the statue is your kingdom.

"After you there will arise another kingdom, not so great as yours. It will be like the silver chest and arms of the statue. And after that kingdom, there will arise a third kingdom, like the bronze in the statue. That kingdom will rule the whole world.

"Finally a fourth kingdom will rise up. It will be as strong as iron, and it will rule the whole earth. That fourth kingdom will be a divided kingdom, as the feet of the statue were part iron and part clay. That kingdom will be partly strong and partly weak.

"While that last kingdom is still standing, the God of heaven will set up his kingdom. His kingdom will be small at first, like the stone. It will shatter all earthly kingdoms, as the stone shattered the statue. All earthly kingdoms, even the greatest, will pass away. But the kingdom of God will fill the earth and last forever.

"The great God has shown the king what will happen in the future. I've told you exactly what you dreamed, and I've given you the correct interpretation."

Nebuchadnezzar was so impressed, he bowed down in front of Daniel and worshiped him. Then he gave orders for sacrifices and incense to be offered to Daniel.

"Truly," he said, "your God is the God of gods, King of kings, the one who reveals secrets. I know this because you've been able to explain the mystery of my dream."

Then Nebuchadnezzar gave Daniel rich gifts and great honors. He made Daniel ruler of the province of Babylon and head of all the wise men.

Daniel asked the king to put Shadrach, Meshach, and Abednego in charge of the province, so he could remain at court near the king.

Rescue from the Fiery Furnace

Daniel 3

ONE time King Nebuchadnezzar had a great statue made, a giant image covered with gold. He had it set up on the plain of Dura, near the city of Babylon. The statue was ninety feet high and nine feet wide, and it towered above the plain.

Then the king ordered all his officials to come to a special ceremony to set the image apart for worship. The satraps, governors, commissioners, treasurers, judges, constables, and other imperial officials gathered together and stood in front of the statue.

"People of all nations, races, and languages!" cried the royal herald. "As soon as you hear the sound of the trumpets and the music of the flutes and harps and drums, you must bow down and worship the golden image. Anyone who doesn't bow down will immediately be taken and thrown into a fiery furnace!"

As soon as they heard the blast of the trumpet and the sound of the music, all the people bowed down and worshiped the statue.

Then some Chaldeans went up to the king and said, "O king, live forever! You have issued an order, but not everyone has obeyed. There are some Jews whom you put in charge of the province of Babylon—their names are Shadrach, Meshach, and Abednego. They're disobeying your order. They're not worshiping your gods. They refuse to bow down to the golden statue."

Nebuchadnezzar was furious. He sent for Shadrach, Meshach, and Abednego and said to them, "Is it true that you refuse to worship the golden image that I have set up? I'll give you another chance. When you hear the music, you must bow down and worship. If you do, then everything will be fine. But if you don't, you'll be thrown into the fiery furnace. Where is the god who is able to save you from my power?"

"O king," answered Shadrach, Meshach, and Abednego, "we won't answer your question. If the God we serve is able to save us from you and your furnace, then he will save us. But if not, O king, you may be sure that we won't serve your gods or bow down to your golden image."

Then Nebuchadnezzar lost his temper. He glared at Shadrach, Meshach, and Abednego with pure hatred. He ordered his servants to heat the furnace seven times hotter than usual. He commanded the strongest men in his army to tie up the three Jews and throw them into the fiery furnace.

They were tied up with all their clothes on, and then they were thrown into the furnace. The furnace was so hot, the flames leaping out of the top killed the men who were carrying Shadrach, Meshach, and Abednego. Then Shadrach,

Meshach, and Abednego fell into the furnace.

Nebuchadnezzar stood in front of the furnace and looked through the ground level opening. Suddenly he leaped to his feet, amazed.

"Didn't we throw in three men, tied with ropes?" he asked his officials.

"Certainly, O king," they answered.

"Look!" he cried. "I see four men walking around in the fire! They're not tied up, and they don't seem hurt. The fourth man looks like a god!"

Nebuchadnezzar went up to the door of the furnace and called out, "Shadrach! Meshach! Abednego! Servants of the Most High God! Come out! Come here!"

And from the middle of the fire out walked Shadrach, Meshach, and Abednego.

All the king's officials crowded around to look at the three men. None of their clothes were burned. Not a hair on their heads was singed. They didn't even smell like smoke. The fire hadn't touched them.

"Praise to the God of Shadrach, Meshach, and Abednego!" cried Nebuchadnezzar. "He sent his angel to rescue his faithful servants. They disobeyed the royal command and risked their lives rather than serve any god except their own God.

"Now I command the people of every nation, race, and language: Do not speak disrespectfully of the God of Shadrach, Meshach, and Abednego. Anyone who does will be torn to pieces, and his

154

house will be torn down. There is no other god who can rescue like this!"

Then the king promoted Shadrach, Meshach, and Abednego to even higher positions in his government.

31

How God Humbled a Proud King

Daniel 4

NEBUCHADNEZZAR was at home in his palace, enjoying his comfort and his wealth. One night he dreamed a frightening dream; he saw terrifying visions that he didn't understand.

The next morning he ordered all the wise men of Babylon to come and tell him what his dream meant. But none of the magicians, enchanters, astrologers, and wizards could explain the king's dream.

Finally Daniel arrived, and Nebuchadnezzar said to him, "I know that the Spirit of God is in you. You can understand all mysteries. You tell me the meaning of my dream.

"While I was sleeping," said the king, "I saw a huge tree growing in the middle of the earth. It grew higher and higher until it reached heaven. The tree was so tall, it could be seen from the ends of the earth. Its leaves were lovely, and it bore enough fruit to feed the whole world. Wild animals rested in its shade; birds built nests in its branches.

"Then I saw an angel coming down from heaven. 'Chop down the tree,' he shouted. 'Cut off its branches. Strip off its leaves and throw away its fruit. Drive away the animals and birds. Just leave the stump in the ground with an iron ring around it. Leave it there in the field with the grass.'

"Then the angel said, 'Now let the rain fall on it. Let him live outdoors like an animal. Let his mind be changed from a human mind to the mind of an animal. And let these things go on for seven years!

"Then the angel said, 'The Watchers have decided these things must be, so that people everywhere will know that God the Most High rules over human kingdoms. He gives power to anyone he chooses.'

"That was my dream," said Nebuchadnezzar. "Now tell me what it means. None of the other wise men can tell me. But you can, for the Spirit of God is in you."

Daniel hesitated for a moment, for his thoughts frightened him.

"Don't let the dream upset you," said the king.

"My lord," answered Daniel, "May the dream be applied to your enemies, and its meaning to your foes!"

Then he explained the dream. "The tree that grew so tall that it reached the sky—that tree, O king, is you. For you have grown so great that your power extends to the ends of the earth.

"The angel that came down from heaven was speaking the command that God has given concerning you. He has passed sentence on you. You will be driven away from human society. You'll live with the wild animals and eat grass like an ox. You'll sleep outdoors, and the rain will fall on you.

"All these things will last for seven years, until the time that you admit that God the Most High rules over all human kingdoms and gives power to anyone he chooses.

"The stump you saw left in the ground with an iron ring around it—that means your kingdom will survive. You will become king again when you admit that God has power over all earthly kingdoms.

"Now, O king, please take my advice. In order to be saved from your sins, do what is right. Show kindness to the poor. Then you'll live a long and peaceful life."

Nebuchadnezzar's dream came true. One day

just a year later he was strolling on the roof of
his palace, saying to himself, "O Babylon! How
great this city is! And I'm the one who built it up,
with my power, to show my glory and my
majesty!"

As soon as he said this, a voice spoke to him
from heaven. "King Nebuchadnezzar, listen.
Your kingdom is being taken away from you!"

Immediately Nebuchadnezzar went out of his
mind and began acting like an animal. He was
driven away from human society. He lived outdoors with the wild animals. He ate grass like an
ox. His hair grew as long as eagles' feathers, and
his fingernails grew as long as birds' claws.

Just seven years later, as Nebuchadnezzar was looking up to heaven, his mind returned. Then he praised God the Most High, and he gave honor and glory to the everliving God.

Nebuchadnezzar's kingdom was restored to him with even more power and honor. And he honored the King of heaven, the God whose kingdom will last forever, the God who has the power to humble the greatest kings.

The Writing on the Wall

Daniel 5

NEBUCHADNEZZAR'S great empire remained powerful as long as he lived. But after reigning for forty-four years, he died, and the kings who followed him were weak.

The international situation became dangerous. In the East, the Medes and the Persians rose to power under the leadership of Cyrus. During the reign of Nabonidus, Cyrus made plans to attack the Babylonian empire and to invade the city of Babylon itself.

Then Nabonidus left Babylon for a few months

and put his son Belshazzar in charge of his kingdom.

One night King Belshazzar gave a great banquet for a thousand of his noblemen. As they were drinking wine together, he ordered his servants to bring in the gold and silver cups and bowls that Nebuchadnezzar had taken from the temple in Jerusalem. Belshazzar wanted the cups and bowls so he and his nobles, his wives and his girlfriends could drink from them.

As soon as they were brought in, the king and his friends drank their wine and praised their gods, gods made of gold and silver, bronze and iron, wood and stone.

Suddenly a human hand appeared. It began writing on the white plaster wall of the banquet hall. The light from the lamps shone on the wall, so the king could see the hand as it wrote.

Belshazzar was so frightened when he saw the hand that he turned pale. His legs felt weak and his knees began to shake.

He shouted for his enchanters, astrologers, and wizards. When they came in, he said to them, "Whoever can read this writing and tell me what it means will be dressed in robes of royal purple. He will wear a solid gold necklace. He will become the third most powerful person in the kingdom."

The wise men of Babylon crowded forward, eager to win the prize. But none of them could read the writing on the wall or tell the king what it meant.

The king was so upset, his face became even paler. The nobles didn't know what to do.

Then the queen mother, who had heard what was going on, came into the banquet hall.

"O king, live forever!" she said. "Don't be upset. There's a man in your kingdom who has the Spirit of God in him. This man used to be famous for his wisdom. Nebuchadnezzar made him head of all the magicians, enchanters, astrologers, and wizards. This man has an extraordinary mind, with great skill in interpreting dreams and solving riddles. You should send for him at once. His name is Daniel. Send for Daniel, and he'll tell you what all this means!"

Belshazzar sent for Daniel, and when he arrived, the king said to him, "Are you the same Daniel whom Nebuchadnezzar brought from Judah? I've heard that the Spirit of God is in you, and that you are extremely wise. I've heard that you can interpret dreams and explain mysteries.

"None of my magicians can read this writing on the wall. If you can read it and tell me what it means, I'll have you dressed in robes of royal purple; I'll put a chain of gold around your neck; and I'll make you the third most powerful man in the kingdom."

"Keep your gifts for yourself," answered Daniel. "Give your rewards to someone else. I'll read the writing and tell the king what it means.

"O king, the Most High God gave Nebuchadnezzar a great kingdom with so much power and glory that people of all nations, races, and languages were afraid of him. Nebuchadnezzar had power of life and death over his subjects.

"But he became proud and boastful. So he was removed from his throne; he lost his glory. He was driven away from human society to live like an animal until he admitted that God the Most High rules over all human kingdoms and can give them to anyone he chooses.

"But you, O king, have not humbled yourself, even though you knew what happened to Nebuchadnezzar. Instead, you rebelled against the Lord of heaven. You brought in the cups and bowls that were taken from the Lord's temple in Jerusalem. You and your friends drank wine from them while you praised your idols—those gods who can't see or hear or understand.

"But you didn't honor the God who controls your life, the God who has control over everything you do. That's why God has sent the hand to write these words.

"And this is what the writing says: MENE, MENE, TEKEL, UPHARSIN.

"And this is what the words mean: MENE means numbered. God has numbered the years of your kingdom and brought it to an end.

"TEKEL means weighed. God has weighed you on the scales, and you are too light.

"UPHARSIN means divided. God has divided your kingdom. He has taken it from you and given it to the Medes and the Persians."

Then Belshazzar ordered his servants to dress Daniel in a robe of royal purple and to put a chain of gold around his neck. He made Daniel the third most powerful person in the kingdom.

That same night Belshazzar, king of Babylon, was killed, and the Medes and the Persians took over his kingdom.

33

Daniel in the Lions' Den

Daniel 6

DARIUS, king of Persia, decided to reorganize his empire. He appointed administrators called satraps to rule each province, and he put three men over the satraps. One of these three men was Daniel.

Daniel did such a good job that the king began to consider putting him in charge of the other officials.

They found out what the king was thinking, and they were so jealous, they looked for an excuse to get Daniel into trouble. But Daniel was dependable, honest, and faithful. They couldn't find anything wrong with his work.

"We'll never find an excuse for ruining Daniel," they said to each other. "Let's attack him through his religion."

After plotting together, and then they went to the king, "King Darius, live forever!" they said. "We've talked it over, and we agree that the king should issue a new order. For the next thirty days, no one should be allowed to ask for anything from any god or man except the king. Anyone who disobeys this law should be thrown into a pit filled with lions.

"Now, O king, issue the order and sign it, so it will become law—a law of the Medes and Persians which can never be changed."

King Darius liked this suggestion, so he issued the order and signed it into law.

When Daniel heard about the new law, he paid no attention to it. He kept going home three times every day to pray to his God. Every day he went to an upstairs room in his house with windows that faced toward Jerusalem. There he prayed, asking his God for different things and offering him praises.

Daniel's enemies walked past his house and looked through the window. When they saw him praying, they went to the king and said, "O king, didn't you just sign an order forbidding anyone for the next thirty days to request anything from any god or man except you? Anyone who disobeys this law must be thrown into the lions' den."

"Yes," answered the king. "That's the law. And a law of the Medes and Persians can never be changed."

"O king," said Daniel's enemies, "that man Daniel, an exile from Judah, is ignoring your law. He prays to his God three times a day."

When the king heard this he was upset. He tried all day to find a way in which he could save Daniel.

That evening Daniel's enemies returned to the king and said, "O king, you know that it is the law of the Medes and Persians that no royal order can be changed."

So the king gave orders for Daniel to be taken and thrown into the pit filled with lions.

"May your God, whom you serve so faithfully, come and rescue you!" the king said to Daniel.

Then a stone was placed over the opening of the pit, and the king put his royal seal on it, so no one could rescue Daniel.

The king returned to his palace, but that night he was unable to eat or sleep.

Early the next morning the king got up and hurried out to the lions' den. As he came near the pit, he shouted out anxiously, "Daniel, servant of the living God! Was your God, whom you serve so faithfully, able to save you from the lions?"

"O king, live forever!" cried Daniel. "My God sent his angel to shut the lions' mouths. They haven't hurt me. God did this because he saw that I was innocent. Now, O king, don't you see that I am innocent of doing you any harm?"

The king was thrilled to hear Daniel's voice, and he ordered his men to release him. After Daniel was pulled out of the pit, the king's servants checked him for signs of injury. They couldn't find any, for Daniel had trusted his God to save him.

Then the king commanded that the men who had accused Daniel should be thrown into the same pit, along with their families. Before they reached the bottom, the lions pounced on them and tore them to pieces.

King Darius wrote to the people of his empire, saying.

Peace be with you! I hereby command
    that every nation in my empire honor
    and respect the God of Daniel.
He is the living God, the everlasting.

His kingdom will never be destroyed;
    his rule will never end.

He saves and he rescues;
    he performs miracles
        in heaven and on earth.
He rescued Daniel
    from the power of the lions!

34

Daniel Sees Beasts and Horns and Gabriel

Daniel 7—9

IN the first year that Belshazzar was king of Babylon, Daniel had a terrifying dream. He wrote down what he saw, but he didn't tell anyone about it.

In his dream Daniel saw four huge beasts coming up out of the ocean. The first beast looked like a lion with eagle's wings. The second looked like a bear. The third beast was like a leopard with four heads and wings.

The fourth beast was a great monster with powerful iron teeth and bronze claws and ten horns. In his dream Daniel saw a little horn growing up among the others, a horn with eyes and a mouth that was bragging. The little horn was making war against the people of God.

Then Daniel saw a heavenly throne and an Ancient One sitting on the throne. The Ancient One's robe was as white as snow, and the hair on his head was like pure wool. The throne was resting on wheels of burning fire, and the throne itself was made of fiery flames. A great stream of fire poured out from the throne.

Then Daniel saw hundreds of thousands of heavenly beings waiting on the Ancient One. He saw the heavenly court meeting to try cases and the heavenly record books being opened.

Someone who looked like a human being was coming with the clouds of heaven. This son of man went up to the Ancient One, and the Ancient One gave him authority, honor, and power. People of all nations, races, and languages served this man, and his rule lasted forever.

In his dream Daniel went up to one of the angels and asked what was going on. What did these things mean?

The angel explained, "The four huge beasts are four kingdoms that will rise to power on earth. The fourth beast is a monstrous kingdom that will conquer the whole world. The ten horns are the ten kings of that kingdom. The little horn is a new king who will rise up and overthrow the others. He will speak against God the Most High, and he'll conquer God's people. He'll try to destroy true religion, and the saints of God will be in his power.

"But then," said the angel, "the heavenly court will judge that wicked king. They'll see that he loses his power. His kingdom will be destroyed. Then the power and the glory of all the kingdoms on earth will be given to the people of God. Their kingdom will last forever."

About two years later Daniel saw another vision. He saw a male sheep with two long horns. This ram was butting in every direction, and no animal could escape its power. Then Daniel saw a male goat come rushing out of the west. The goat had a great horn on its forehead. It went up to the ram and attacked it, knocked it down, and broke off both its horns.

Then Daniel saw the goat becoming more powerful. Just when it was at the height of its power, its great horn snapped off and four new horns grew up in its place.

One of the four new horns was enormous. It attacked the heavenly army; it even attacked the commander of the heavenly army. It attacked true religion and stopped worship at God's temple. It set up an evil idol on the altar of the temple.

Then Daniel saw someone who looked like a young man, and he heard a voice calling, "Gabriel, reveal to him the meaning of this vision."

Gabriel went up to Daniel, and Daniel fell down to the ground in terror.

"O man," said Gabriel, "understand this. The vision shows the time of the end of history."

Then Gabriel touched Daniel and lifted him to his feet. "Listen," he said. "I'll tell you what's going to happen in the time of God's anger. The ram with the two horns is the kingdom of the Medes and the Persians. The goat is the kingdom of the Greeks. The great horn is the first ruler of the Greek empire. The four new horns are the four kingdoms that will rise when that empire is divided.

"In the last days of the Greek kings, after they have committed all their crimes, a proud king will rise; he will brag and plan enormous evil. He'll attack God's people, but he will be destroyed when he challenges God himself. These dreadful things will go on until the temple is re-stored.

"Meanwhile, Daniel, you must keep this vision a secret. It will be many years before these things come to pass."

Daniel fainted with fright, and for several days he was sick. The vision confused him, for he didn't understand it.

A few years later Daniel saw another vision. He was at home, studying the prophecies of Jeremiah and praying to the Lord to help him understand what he was reading.

"Hear my prayer, O Lord," said Daniel. Then he suddenly saw Gabriel flying down toward him.

"Daniel," said Gabriel, "I've come to give you understanding. God has answered your prayer. He loves you very much, and he has sent me to reveal a secret to you. He is going to cause Jeremiah's prophecies to come true. Crimes will stop, sins will be forgiven, justice will be es-tablished, and the temple will be rededicated.

"Now listen carefully. From the time the com-mand is given to rebuild Jerusalem until God's anointed prince comes, seven weeks of years will pass. Jerusalem will be rebuilt inside and out. It will stand for sixty-two weeks of years, but those years will be a time of troubles.

"At the end of that time, an anointed one will be killed, and the soldiers of a powerful ruler will destroy the city and the temple. That ruler will set up a shameful idol on the altar of the temple. It will stay there until God destroys that ruler."

Daniel didn't understand what Gabriel was telling him, but he wrote down everything he heard.

35

Secrets About the Future

Daniel 10—12

WHEN Daniel was an old man, he saw a vision that explained to him the meaning of the end of history. He fasted for three weeks to prepare himself for a revelation. He didn't eat any rich food or meat, and he didn't drink any wine.

Then one day, while he was standing on the bank of the river, Daniel saw a vision of a heavenly being, someone who looked like a man. He was dressed in white linen and wore a belt of pure gold. His body was shining like a jewel. His face was as bright as lightning. His eyes looked like flaming torches. His arms and legs were gleaming like polished bronze.

Daniel was the only one who saw this vision. The people with him didn't see anything, but they were so frightened, they ran away and hid.

Then Daniel heard a voice that sounded like the roar of the ocean. When he heard the voice of the heavenly being, he was so frightened, he fainted.

He lay on the ground until a hand took hold of him and raised him up to his hands and knees. He saw an angel standing beside him.

"Daniel," said the angel, "God loves you very much. Now listen carefully to what I say. Stand up. I've been sent to give you some news."

Daniel stood up, still trembling with fear.

"Don't be afraid," said the angel. "From the first day of your fast, God listened to your prayer. That's why I'm here. The guardian angel of Persia opposed me for three weeks, but Michael, one of the chief angels, came to my rescue. I left Michael fighting the angel of Persia. Now I'm going to tell you what will happen to your people in the future."

While the angel was speaking, Daniel kept his face down, and he didn't say a word.

Then the angel touched Daniel's lips, and Daniel opened his mouth and said, "When I saw you, my lord, I was overcome with terror and weakness. How can I speak to you? I've lost all my strength."

The angel touched Daniel again. "Don't be afraid," he said. "God loves you very much. You're safe. Be strong and brave."

As the angel was speaking, Daniel began to feel strong and brave. "All right," he said to the angel. "Now you may speak, for you have given me the courage I need to hear what you have to say."

The angel said, "I'm going to reveal to you what's written in the Book of Truth, God's record of the past and future."

Then he told Daniel, "Three more kings will rule over Persia. Then a fourth king will arise, the richest of them all, and he will attack the Greeks.

"A mighty king will arise in Greece. That king will conquer a great empire, but at the height of his power his kingdom will be divided into four parts, and other men will rule over it. They will fight among themselves for many years.

"Then a new king will arise in the north. He'll destroy everyone who opposes him, even the high priest of the Lord. He'll try to destroy true religion, and he'll attack God's people. His soldiers will ruin the temple. They'll stop the worship services, and then they'll set up a horrible idol, an Abomination of Desolation, on the altar.

"Loyal people will oppose that king, and wise teachers will lead the people against him. But they'll be tested by fire and sword. God's people will receive a little help, but some of their leaders will be killed.

"The wicked king will set himself up as higher than any god, even the God of gods. On the altar of the true God, that king will offer gold and silver jewels to a new god. But the time will come for the end of this wicked man. He will perish, and no one will help him.

"Then the great angel Michael will appear, and there will be a time of troubles. But your people will be saved. All those whose names are written in God's Book of Life will be saved. Many of those who are in their graves will live again. Some will wake to everlasting life, while others will suffer everlasting shame. The wise leaders of God's people will shine like the brightness of heaven.

Those who have taught the people the ways of justice will shine forever, like the stars.

"As for you, Daniel, keep these words secret. Seal the book until the time of the end. In the meantime, many people will leave true religion. Evil will increase.

"Now go your way, Daniel. The words are secret and sealed until the time of the end. Blessed are the people who remain faithful during the time of persecution.

"Now go your way and take your rest. At the end of time, you will rise for your reward."

THE WORLD OF EZEKIEL, EZRA, AND ESTHER

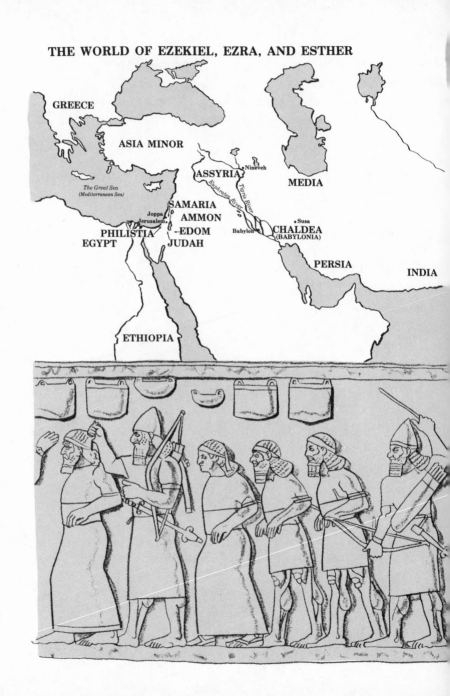

GREECE

ASIA MINOR

ASSYRIA • Nineveh

The Great Sea
(Mediterranean Sea)

MEDIA

Euphrates River

Tigris River

SAMARIA
Joppa• AMMON
Jerusalem•
PHILISTIA —EDOM
EGYPT JUDAH

Babylon• CHALDEA • Susa
(BABYLONIA)

PERSIA

INDIA

ETHIOPIA

Eve Bowers MacMaster graduated from the Pennsylvania State University and George Washington University. She also studied at Harvard University and Eastern Mennonite Seminary. She has taught in the Bible department at Eastern Mennonite College and in the history department at James Madison University, both located in Harrisonburg, Virginia.

Eve visited many of the places mentioned in the Bible while she was serving as a Peace Corps Volunteer in Turkey.

Eve and her husband, Richard, live near Harrisonburg, Virginia, with their chidren, Sam, Tom, and Sarah.